In Our Lives First

MEDITATIONS FOR COUNSELORS
VOLUME 2

Diane Mandt Langberg, PhD

Langberg, Monroe, & Associates
Jenkintown, Pennsylvania

Langberg, Monroe & Associates
512 West Avenue
Jenkintown, PA 19046
www.dianelangberg.com
info@dianelangberg.com

Book Layout ©2017 BookDesignTemplates.com

Ordering Information:
Quantity sales. Special discounts are available on quantity purchases by corporations, associations, and others. For details, contact the "Special Sales Department" at the address above.

In Our Lives First, Second Volume/ Diane Langberg. —1st ed.
ISBN 979-8-218-12411-3

Contents

Dedication

To all the courageous men and women who have known the crushing of trauma and refused to be defined by it. You have been my teachers and I'm exceedingly grateful. Walking with you has been an honor.

Many thanks to Evangeline Hsieh whose hard work, fine mind, and grace make this second version possible.

Forward

Many Christian counselors are feeling the powerful impact of evil and the suffering of others on their own lives. They are hungry to know how to withstand that impact without being misshapen by it. I too have wrestled with this, seeking to understand what happens to us as we sit day after day with suffering.

We humans are image bearers. The people and events of our lives shape us. We bear the image of our own histories, the characteristics of our parents. Our clients often have imprints of abuse, violence, and neglect. Decades ago, I worked with a woman who grew up with extreme neglect, violence, and sexual abuse. Her fear was a palpable force in the room. Her body literally curled up as she cowered in my presence. She bore the image of her history.

Human beings, over time, reflect the things that have been imprinted on them, things they have taken into their very substance. We become like that which we habitually reflect. If you grow up with a violent father, recognizable pieces of him will eventually show up, one way or another. Recognizable bits of one soul, over time, begin to show up in another. So as counselors you and I certainly impact our clients. They bear the image, to one degree or another, of sitting with us. Who we are with

1

them can have a profound impact. What we often fail to recognize is that our clients shape us as well.

I have been profoundly shaped by decades of working with trauma. I have been altered by the many stories of abuse and trauma emanating from the church and Christian organizations. I have been shaken by the failure of God's people to call things by their right name and to bring light to darkness no matter where it is found. All these have changed me. As a young therapist I believed this work was for the purpose of helping others change. It is. Little did I know that one of those people would be me. We follow one called Man of Sorrows and acquainted with grief. He too has been shaped and eternally changed by walking among us and bearing our anguish.

You can only do God's work through him, as he does his work in you. We cannot do the work of the Redeemer unless he first does his redemptive work in us. Let the work expose you to yourself. And allow that exposure to take you to the Cross with a heart that pleads for God's redemptive work in you. Caregiving is a difficult work. The work of God moves into the lives of the diseased and dying, the afflicted, the brokenhearted, the mourning, and the captive. We prefer moving into health, wholeness, joy, and freedom. We must bow to the work of redemption in us, for it is only as He makes us like his Son that we will be willing and fit to move into those places we most want to avoid. I have had to learn to bow down and ask him to do his work in me so his work through me might be accomplished.

Hence this second little book of meditations – thought borne out of sitting with sorrow and suffering. It is, as with the first book, borne out of a lifetime in the therapist's chair which has challenged me, changed me, and increased my thirst for the one who is Living Water in a dry and thirsty land.

Week 1

Soldiers of the Kingdom

As counselors, we are particularly attuned to news of the suffering of soldiers, both physically and psychologically. We have been called upon to offer our services to those who are struggling with the trauma of war and re-entry. The Veterans Administration and many ministries that serve our armed forces have asked for us to step up. If you think about it, in some ways we have been asked to come forward as an army of caregivers and enter the battle of sitting with another's trauma. I am struck, as I think about it, how we have much to learn from those whom we have been called to serve – but then, is that not always the case? We go to help and are helped; we go to teach and are taught; we go to challenge and are challenged as well. May we be good students of these faithful men and women who have entered into war, evil, atrocities, and suffering for the sake of others here and abroad.

Like our soldiers, we have been called to enter the "combat zone." We are the body of Christ, and he has told us in his Word that this world will be full of trouble and tragedies (John 16:33 NASB). He has told us that this whole world lies in the power of the evil one (1 John 5:19 NASB). We are in a place of service in the midst of a war. It requires a willingness to enter into danger, combat, threat, suffering, evil, and darkness. It is the way Jesus went, and we are called to follow Him there. To retreat as the body of Christ from the care of our combat veterans, or others who suffer from trauma, is to retreat from being a faithful soldier of Jesus Christ.

Like our troops around the world, we must also realize that the battle is not just out there and against them. There is no them; there is just humanity – people created in the image of God. Even when they are doing evil, hate us, and want us dead – that is still who they are. Furthermore, the war is also not simply out there – it is in here, in my heart and mind as well. It is critical that we remember this, or we are in danger of fighting a good fight in bad ways.

Dealing with evil – done by or to someone, whether in war or in listening to the stories in a counseling office – has great power to work toxins into our souls. Humans are easily contaminated – even when working for a worthy and just cause. We can quickly end up serving our agenda rather than our Master. Absorbing what we sit with or fight against can come too easily. Sometimes the pain goes in mindlessly. We become anesthetized to it, so we inhale and imbibe the inherent toxins without awareness. Blinded, we fail to see the impact of the battle on our own hearts and minds. From there, we end up serving the endless needs of others without caring for ourselves, or we obey the institution without question rather than our God. Perhaps we use unholy means to achieve what we believe to be a holy goal. Working to restore those who have been traumatized by the evil and suffering in this world can easily lead us to cease following our Master, thinking that the fight is only against what is out there. It is indeed, but we must never forget it is also ever and always within us as well.

Good soldiers obey their commanders. We follow a Commander who has crossed an infinite divide to welcome us with his great grace. He is the Man of Sorrows, and we are to follow him without question into the sorrows and suffering of others. While we do that, we must be clear that he is the one we follow and our service for him is only of value to him when his name and character are honored in our lives. Those soldiers now coming home entered battle in the name of the United States and this nation calls them to a certain standard in their lives. You and I go out under a far greater name than that of the United States. We go out under the banner of the Lord Jesus Christ. Our work with the suffering is most certainly to look like him in word and deed. However, he has made clear that his kingdom is the kingdom of the heart, and so our hearts and minds must be utterly his as we follow him immediately and without question.

For further thought:

Take some time to pray and reflect on the work you are doing in the combat zone God has called you to.

> *"Every Christian has to partake of what is the essence of the Incarnation; he must bring the thing down into flesh and blood realities and work it out through the fingertips."*
>
> **Oswald Chambers**[1]

---

[1] Oswald Chambers, *My Utmost for His Highest* (New York, NY: Dodd Mead & Co., 1935), March 6. Used with permission; see References.

The Different Parts We Play

In discussing the whole area of lay counseling, it is crucial we lay down a basis for such a ministry from the Scriptures. Any time we speak about ministry in the body of Christ, we must do so within the context of the Word of God.

Paul said, "For even as the body is one and yet has many members, and all the members of the body, though they are many, are one body, so also is Christ" (1 Corinthians 12:12 NASB). The body of Christ is a unit. We are individual members of the one body of Christ. We are all bound up together. If you or I fail, it is not an isolated fall. Our fall impacts the whole body. In a physical body, if the leg gives way, it is not just the leg that falls down. The whole body goes with it. "For none of us lives to himself alone and none of us dies to himself alone" (Romans 14:7 NIV). We are a unit, you and me. My sin and suffering impact you, and your sin and suffering affect me. Whether we like each other or not, whether we live close

9

together or far apart, we are many parts that form one body.

We cannot argue our way out of the body. We cannot say because we are less important, therefore, we are not a part. We cannot say that because others are not like us, they are not a part of the body. We cannot say that because someone is weak or powerless or unattractive, that they are not part of the body. We do not decide who is part of the body and who is not. We do not decide what place each one has in the body. "God has arranged the parts in the body, every one of them, just as he wanted them to be" (1 Corinthians 12:18 NIV).

I fear that we are often discontent with the work of God. We do not like the part we have been given. It is too big; it is too small. We feel stuck out on the end of the body, and we would rather be in the middle. We do not like being feet because we get walked on. We do not like being eyes because we see things we would rather not see. We prefer to be in a higher position when we have been given a lower one. Sometimes we do not mind the part we were given, but we are not happy with the arrangements of the other parts around us. We feel stuck with the less desirable parts of the body. We are eyes that live with those who cannot see. We are ears that live with those who cannot hear. Rather than understanding what others do and how we need what they do, we get impatient and annoyed because they cannot do what we do.

When Christ was here in the flesh, he had a body. Every part of that sacred body lived in obedience to God. If it had not, we would not have a Redeemer. His face was set toward Jerusalem. His ears were attuned to the voice of God and to the suffering of people. His hands healed and became scarred. His mouth taught truth boldly and graciously. His feet walked the way of the Cross. His side was pierced for our transgressions.

Now Jesus has returned to heaven and is no longer here in the flesh. But he still has a body. You and I are that body which, like his fleshly body, is meant to do the redemptive work of God in this world. If any part of the fleshly body of Christ had failed, you and I would be gravely affected. Do we see that any time a part of the body of Christ fails to do the work God intended in its assigned place, you and I will suffer?

We can draw several implications from the above truths. First, we cannot sin in isolation. Whenever you and I sin, we sin not only against God himself, but also against the body. We fool ourselves into thinking it will not affect anyone else. That makes any sinfulness on our part far more serious than the act itself. Second, we are seriously impacted by one another's suffering. Suffering reverberates throughout the body. To be part of the body is to enter into a relationship that will bring on us the suffering of others. Third, each part is crucial according to God. Importance is determined by participation in the body, not by position. There is no such thing as an unimportant part of the body.

What does this mean for those of us in the counseling ministries of the body of Christ? We are pastors, social workers, psychologists, professional counselors, psychiatrists, and lay counselors. Paul tells us that there are varieties of gifts, ministries, and effects, but they all emanate from the same Spirit, the same Lord, the same God who works all things in all persons (1 Corinthians

12:4-6 NASB). We are all necessary, all important. We should treat each with respect and honor. We should continually be looking for ways to work together and support one another. Our assignments were given to us by God, and it is he who works in and through each of us to care for the members of his body here on earth. Such an arrangement allows no room for pride, competition, jostling for position, or seeking for fame. Rather, each member should be characterized by humility and service to others.

For further thought:

How has God gifted you as part of His body? Do you feel dissatisfied with your role in any way?

"If we will steadfastly believe that everything in the world which is in pain and everything which has power, is God's, and shall be used by Him, the one for the sake of the other, this shall surely change the way of our feet, and all the world around to our eyes."

George Adam Smith[2]

---

[2] George Adam Smith, *The Expositor's Bible: The Book of Isaiah Volumes I and II* (London: Hodder and Stoughton Publishers, 1890), 295.

The Body of Christ

The principles found in Scripture about how to live together in the body of Christ lead to the following conclusions:

1) As part of the body of Christ, I never function in isolation. Believers serve as a unit. What we do and who we are in public and private, impacts the rest of the body. There is no such thing as, "Oh, it won't hurt anybody."

2) As part of the body of Christ, I am to live in subjection to others. Your choices, struggles, and sin will impact me and who you are will affect me. Protecting myself from tragedies, struggles with sin, and adversity is not supported by Scripture.

3) As part of the body of Christ, I see that I *need* the weak, for I am just like them, and we all need the strength of Christ. As a result, I will walk with others humbly. Superiority or favoritism has no place in the body of Christ.

4) As part of the body of Christ, I will know that honor is bestowed as *God* directs, not according to the principles of our worldly environment.

5) As part of the body of Christ, I am called to demonstrate his example, no matter who you are or what you do.

If we instill these principles into our lives, we will be transformed. We must realize that we cannot sin without damaging each other. Knowing this will keep us on our knees before God. And knowing we are subject to one another's struggles and sins will help us to intercede for one another. When others are weak, we must allow the impact of that weakness to drive us to Christ, seeking more of him so we might become more like him. When others are not honorable according to the world's standards, we will honor them, knowing all of life is lived in the presence of the Unseen, and his claims far exceed the paltry claims of this world. When others are not presentable, we will seek out the character of God in order to demonstrate to them who He is.

As counselors, pastors, and lay advisors in the Body of Christ, our work with others who are suffering requires us to live out these principles. We are called to suffer with the suffering. To be a part of the body is to enter a costly commitment, for it means inviting the suffering of others into our lives. We also know that the greater the suffering, the greater the time commitment on our part, but entering into the suffering of others is truly redemptive for both parties. You see, if we allow ourselves to be open, the suffering of others gives us more of Christ.

God designed the body. No human would have fashioned it the way God did. But he knew it was what we needed, and he knew it would work. And God's design teaches us more about our Redeemer who voluntarily became an integral part of us. Was not the Word made flesh? Did He not treat the weak, the dishonorable, and the unpresentable as important and worthy? While we were still sinners, did not Christ die for the ungodly? And who has suffered with us? Did He not take up our griefs and carry our sorrows?

He, who is omnipotent, became weak. He, who alone is worthy, was dishonored. He, who is Beauty, became unpresentable. He is our Head, and the body that does not follow its head becomes sick. Our Head calls us to demonstrate his love to others. To be a part of the body is an inestimable privilege because it means we are a part of Christ. And this is a costly commitment for he walks among the sick, the tormented, the diseased, the despairing, and the sinful. Such a journey will expose our selfishness, our prejudices, our impatience, our criticisms, our preferences, and our lack of courage. We may discover we are not the person we thought we were. Perhaps we think we are patient, loving, and merciful. But if we follow the Lord and commit ourselves to serving the weak, the dishonorable, and the unpresentable, we will surely cry out to our Redeemer. And he will respond to our weakness and insufficiency by lovingly filling us with himself so we might be more like our Lord to this world.

For further thought:

Take a moment to reflect and meditate on the five principles listed at the beginning of this devotional. Which of these stood out to you? Why?

"The Potter has a thought in mind for His clay and He alone is able to transfer His thought to the clay. Does the Potter gain anything in the clay? Surely yes, for through the clay He can give to others a vision of that which is in His mind which cannot be seen save through such a vehicle. God gains in humanity an instrument of revelation."

G. Campbell Morgan[3]

---

[3] G. Campbell Morgan, *Studies in the Prophecy of Jeremiah* (Grand Rapids, MI: Fleming H. Revell, Co., 1955), 117. Used with permission; see References.

Bringing the Extraordinary into Flesh and Blood

Going to places of great tragedy and death is rarely seen as a privilege. I have, however, found it to be so. As a psychologist who has worked with various kinds of trauma for many years, I have learned many eternal lessons in the darkest of places. Ground Zero is one of those.

Television shots cannot begin to convey the magnitude of the devastation. The stench hits you in the face as you exit the van. A sea of gray ash rises up with twisted metal shapes protruding in odd ways. The perimeter is filled with buildings, some partly destroyed, others completely. Many of the buildings have melted façades and the images are surreal. On one edge of the rubble stands a little church known as St. Paul's Chapel. It was built in the 1700s and has survived many wars. It also emerged intact on September 11.

The chapel is surrounded by a beautiful wrought iron fence. As we approach the property my eye catches a computer-generated sign taped to the fence, which reads, "Foot Care Inside." A church offering foot care. How like our Lord who "having loved his own who were in the world, he now showed them the full extent of his love...he poured water into a basin and began to wash his disciples' feet" (John 13:1, 5 NIV). There is another sign nearby on the same fence that reads, "Holy Eucharist, noon today." Foot care and communion, what a beautiful pairing! What a picture of the church, bringing the holiest of things alongside acts of mercy in a devastated place...

I was given the opportunity to go into the pit, as the workers call it, and spend some time walking among the workers with a chaplain. I accepted the invitation and arrived dressed in blue jeans and boots. I spent about five hours in the pit with a young woman who had been spending every night during the graveyard shift walking among the men and women, listening to them, encouraging them, and praying for them. The cranes loomed large, and the rescue workers seemed small.

When the cranes stopped, the workers picked up their rakes, shovels, and buckets and went to the area where the cranes had been to dig and rake, looking for signs of humanity. We went with them and stood by while they dug, praying for them. About 3 a.m. I realized a group of them were gathering together and raking. "They must have found something," the young chaplain said. I was overcome with grief. Death was everywhere, physically, emotionally, and spiritually. I looked up and saw a piece of the façade of the World Trade Center rising from the rubble. At the end of it the beams formed three crosses, brilliantly lit by the powerful spotlights. I put my arm around the woman I was with and said, "Look, He is here." And then it hit me, the eternal lesson in the midst of the trauma.

As the people of God, we have in many ways been called to serve as the rescue workers of the world. Surely this world, for all its beauty, looks something like the World Trade Center to our God who sees death destroying what He created. He has called us to enter this dark world and search. The rescue workers would never think of making a permanent home in the ruins. The rubble is not their home. Nor is this world ours. We have been invited into the fellowship of the sufferings of Christ. We are called into the places of darkness and death for that is where He went. He has called us to serve Him in this dark place of death, moving among those who are dead in their trespasses and sins, calling them to life and light. The church is called to bring the holiest of things alongside acts of mercy in a devastated place. We are called to bring the extraordinary (the life of the Son of God) down into flesh and blood, down into the ordinary, under the shadow of the cross. We are called because He whom we love entered the rubble of our world and our lives and experienced all the death of this place that we might know Life. He bore the destruction of the World Trade Center. He bore all the tragedies of this world. He has borne the selfishness and complacency we display when we try to make this rubble our home. Oh, may we see the eternal in the devastation. May we live for the cross rising from the ashes. May we honor the Man of Sorrows by our willingness to walk where He walked, washing feet, and searching among the ruins because He died.

For further thought:

Where in the ordinariness of life can you see Him at work? Where in the suffering can you catch glimpses of Him?

"You can take a negative position; that is, look at him and pass by on the other side of the man. But he who does so perpetuates his pain and is guilty of the continuity of his suffering. In the presence of humans there is one alternative: shall I do good or shall I do ill? The alternatives of heaven admit of no compromises."

G. Campbell Morgan[4]

---

[4] G. Campbell Morgan, *The Gospel According to Mark* (Grand Rapids. MI: Fleming H. Revell, Co., 1927), 60. Used with permission; see References.

Crises Reveal Character

I learned something many years ago from the writings of devotional author Oswald Chambers: *crises reveal character*. When we are put to the test, the hidden resources of our character are revealed exactly. I fear we often think when a crisis comes, we will rise to the occasion. I believe, however, that Chambers is right, for we can only reach something by a repeated experience of it. That which has been repeated, practiced, and habituated in our lives is revealed in the cold light of crises.

We saw this demonstrated in the crisis of Hurricane Katrina. The devastation served as both a backdrop and a spotlight to reveal the character of local governments, the wealthy, the poor, the police, the Church, and the federal government – the character of systems and individuals has been exposed. Much of what was revealed was ugly. Yes, there were stories of heroism and generosity and sacrifice. Such stories shine a kind light on what it means to be human. The horrific stories of abandonment, anarchy, and rage made us angry, ashamed, and shocked. The fact is, Katrina was a crisis of massive proportions, and if Chambers is right, then it merely forced to the front the habits of character that people had developed over the years.

As parents and extended family members age, it creates a crisis – sometimes multiple crises. House space can be stretched beyond capacity and finances as well. Working adults are squeezed between the needs of the older and younger generations, often with jobs thrown into the mix. For many, the loss of a parent extends gradually over the years – failing health, failing mental capacity, and failing finances. As external restraints lessen, some parents seem to dissolve into the worst of themselves with anger, anxiety, and relentless demands. Patience, kindness, and faithfulness become difficult to demonstrate on the road of a long, slow decline in life. Those who once cared for us now need our care and the rewards can seem few for some. Others are caring for parents who, in fact, did not care well for them. It can be a hard place. It can last a long time. It will also give us some glimpses into our spottiness when it comes to looking like Christ. We will be tempted to blame the stress, the demanding parent, or the complicated life we have. Our God says what comes out reveals the heart.

There are two things I think we need to hold close. One is the place of hidden and difficult service and following the Son of Man who came to serve. This is the essence of our faith. The Christian world has a lot of glitz and glamour and fame in it today. That is not the way our Savior went. George Matheson, an old Scottish theologian, has taught me a great deal. He was physically blind, but the eyes of his heart were *clear* and piercing. He once commented: "It has been said that Christianity is a progressive religion; to me its distinctive feature is its *regressiveness*. It is the only religion which goes back to gather up the lost things – the things which have fallen by the way and been left behind... Jesus alone has a message for the weak."[5]

For those who are caring for their own parents, or the aged, the sick, and the blind – please know that you are following the footsteps of the Lord who left glory to do the same. He came, He touched, He blessed, and He sacrificed. He did the ordinary, the small and touched what was not clean. Your tending of others is like Him. Nothing you do is too small for God to notice. Your sacrificial service, your going back, brings delight to His heart.

Second, where the crises of such care do not reveal the habituated character of Jesus Christ, then let His piercing light expose it. Do not run; do not pretend; do not excuse or blame. You see, God does not expose us to shame or condemn us. Such exposure is a call to run to Him so He can give us more of Himself. Sometimes our sacrificial work will reveal ministration, gentleness, sacrificial love, and patience. Other times, it will reveal resentment, judgment, impatience, and neglect. Then what will we do?

---

[5] George Matheson, *Studies of the Portrait of Christ* (London: Hodder and Stoughton., 1902), 108-109.

Dear caregivers, do not forget that your God, who never sleeps, is caring for you in your work with broken lives – whether they are in your counseling office or family. Part of that gracious care is the exposure of where we are not like Him *so that* He can make us more like Himself, which is, in fact, our only joy. May the tragedies that come – whether they are aging minds that descend into dementia, ingratitude, and hostility or suffering, sinning clients – afford an opportunity for this world to see those who name His name and follow the Lamb whithersoever He goes, looking like Him. Moving through this life from dawn until dark, devoting themselves to a life of voluntary sacrifice governed by love.

For further thought:

Think about the crises you have experienced or are currently going through. Bring them in prayer to God.

> *"It is only the loyal soul who believes that God engineers circumstances. We take such liberty with our circumstances, we do not believe God engineers them, although we say we do; we treat the things that happen as though they were in fact engineered by men."*
>
> **Oswald Chambers**[6]

---

[6] Oswald Chambers, *My Utmost for His Highest* (New York, NY: Dodd Mead & Co., 1935), December 18. Used with permission; see References.

Brief Meditation 1

"A man is what his heart makes him. The outer life is but the blossoming of the inner soul and what we call character is but the subtle and silent influence, the odor – fragrant or otherwise – which the soul unconsciously throws out."

Henry Burton[7]

---

[7] Henry Burton, *The Expositor's Bible: The Gospel According to Luke* (London: Hodder and Stoughton Publishers, 1890), 120-121.

Brief Meditation 2

"What our King desires before He ascends the throne of the world is that the world should know Him; and so He comes down among us, to be heard and seen and handled of us, that our hearts may learn His heart and know His love, bewildered by His majesty."

George Adam Smith[8]

---

[8] George Adam Smith, *The Expositor's Bible: The Book of Isaiah Volumes I and II*, 44.

Week 2

The Church as a Sanctuary

In the Old Testament, the Israelites, God's chosen nation, were given regulations both for worship and for an earthly sanctuary. God told Moses to "have them make a sanctuary *for me*, and I will dwell among them" (Exodus 25:8 NIV). Since the coming of Christ, we now have a living tabernacle or sanctuary, for God dwells within his people both individually and corporately. In different ways, the old and the new sanctuaries have both been the dwelling place of God. Scripture is clear about the fact that the place where God dwells is to be a holy place as well as a place of refuge for the poor and oppressed of the earth. The psalmist says, "Lord, who may dwell in your sanctuary? Who may live on your holy hill? He whose walk is blameless and who does what is righteous, who speaks the truth from his heart...who does his neighbor no wrong...who despises a vile man" (Psalm 15:1-4 NIV). The sanctuary of God is to be a holy place that provides a refuge from evil. Surely what characterized the sanctuary made by hands is to be manifested in the tabernacle made by God, the body of his church.

Sadly, instead of manifesting holiness and safety, the dwelling place of God has sometimes mirrored the horror we find in the tribe of Benjamin. In Deuteronomy 33:12 (NIV), Moses pronounces the following blessing on the tribe of Benjamin before his death: "Let the beloved of the Lord rest secure in him, for he shields him all day long, and the one the Lord loves rests between his shoulders." One would think that a group of people so secure and shielded by the Lord God himself would offer that same refuge and security to those who entered their borders. Instead, we find in Judges 19 the horrific story of the rape and death of the Levite's concubine.

In Judges we are told that this particular concubine was angry with the man to whom she was legally attached. In her anger she left him and returned to her father's house. He went after her four months later. After several days, the Levite finally extricated himself and his concubine and began his journey home. It was dangerous to sleep unprotected in the countryside, and the Levite chose to stay in Gibeah, where Benjamites lived.

Although the law of hospitality was strong in the Middle East, it was some time before they were offered shelter. Finally, an old man took them in. Some of the wicked men of the city came pounding on the door later, demanding to have sex with the Levite. The owner of the house felt that would be disgraceful since the Levite was his guest, and instead the owner offered his own virgin daughter and the Levite's concubine. The men would not listen, so finally the concubine was handed out to them by the Levite himself, and they raped and abused her all night long. At dawn when they let her go, she worked her way back to the house where her master was and fell down at the door, her hands on the threshold. Her master's response upon finding her there was to tell her to get up so they could go home. There was no answer; she was dead. He put her across his donkey, took her body home, cut it in twelve pieces, and sent them into all the sections of Israel.

When the rest of Israel learned of the devastation that had occurred, they were shocked, and they all assembled before the Lord in Mizpah. We are told that "the leaders of all the people of the tribes of Israel took their places in the assembly of the people of God" (Judges 20:2 NIV). After hearing the Levite's story, they united as one man against the Benjamites. First, they asked the Benjamites to surrender the men who had committed the abuse. The Benjamites would not listen and chose instead to protect them, exhibiting a misplaced loyalty to the abusers of Gibeah. They chose to fight on behalf of the evil men against their own "brethren the children of Israel" (Judges 20:13, KJV). As a result, Israel went to God at Bethel, the house of God, and asked him what they should do. God directed them to go against the Benjamites.

I think we would expect that if God told Israel to go against the Benjamites, he would give them victory. Instead, the Israelites lost 22,000 men on the battlefield that day. They went to God and wept before him, asking again what to do. God sent them again to fight the

Benjamites. This time they lost eighteen thousand, all armed with swords. In other words, they sent in prepared men and lost them in the fray. A third time they went weeping before the Lord. They fasted and offered sacrifices. Again, they asked whether or not they should go up against their brothers. This time God said yes and promised them victory.

The horrific sin of the Benjamites resulted in brother having to go against brother at great cost to many. It was the only way to "purge the evil" in their midst. The holiness of God demands that the sin be dealt with. Doing so required perpetual seeking after him with tears, fasting, and sacrifices (which meant in part dealing with their own sin). Thousands of innocent men died as a result. The cost was great. God continued to send them into the fight, knowing about that cost. He did not make it easy. The effects of the hideous rape and murder and the Benjamites' attempted protection of the evildoers cost thousands of lives. Had they allowed the perpetrators to be brought to justice, it would have been far less costly to the nation of Israel. Whenever the body of Christ, through denial or actual choice, ignores such sins in its midst, the entire body suffers terribly as a result.

Obedience to God in circumstances such as these is very costly. We in the church of God are engaged in a battle. Scripture makes it abundantly clear that all of life is a battle for those who love God, yet few seem willing to bear it as an occupation. Yes, we will get hurt. Suffering leaves its mark all over those who must endure it. Entering into the suffering of others will also leave a mark. God does not promise that such battles will be without cost. However, as we seek him and weep before him, he will enable us to fight. He will give wisdom so that we do not send people out to be abused. He will grant us open hearts so that no one dies on our thresholds but rather everyone is welcomed in and protected. He will grant us courage to enter the fray, knowing that whatever the cost, the ultimate price has been paid by his Son, enabling all of us to find God as our fortress, our deliverer, our refuge, and our shield. May we as the body of Christ provide sanctuary to others, never causing someone to cry out with David, "I have no refuge; not one cares for my life" (Psalm 142:4, NIV).

For further thought:

Pray for wisdom and courage when we are faced with suffering and battles that may cost us something. Pray that the Church will choose to lean into the hardship that comes with these things, to remain a sanctuary to the vulnerable and suffering.

"That which was at the beginning that alone abides. The woe and grief and cruelty of man to man – these are of time. Love is of eternity. Disbelieve this and your heart will break. Believe it and you can endure."

Amy Carmichael[9]

---

[9] Amy Carmichael, *His Thoughts Said, His Father Said* (Fort Washington, PA: CLC Publications, 1949, 1979), 110. Used with permission; see References.

The Deceived Heart

We all carry a great capacity for deception. The Scriptures say it is the most prevalent and profound characteristic of the human heart and tells us our hearts are unknowable. We are all human; so counselors are human hearts, working alongside other human hearts. *All* such hearts are exceedingly complex and fragile. They are knowable in limited ways and easily damaged.

Deception essentially functions as a narcotic, for it protects us from seeing clearly or feeling that which is painful. A person who is skilled in deception is one who is essentially addicted to deceit. Deception deeply habituates the soul to look at things diametrically opposed to the way God sees, for He is a God of truth. Deception is about hiding, pretending, ignoring, and camouflaging. We use all manner of self-deceptions to protect us from information that would cause us to view ourselves in ways that we do not like. This mechanism enables us to turn a blind eye, commit wrongs, and feel justified when we ought to be facing our failures, abuses, and sins. The maintenance of any destructive pattern in a human life – such as a sex addiction – requires a foundation, an infrastructure. Its cornerstone is deception.

There is a second phenomenon to consider that is also relevant to a discussion of sexual addictions. It is self-injury. Sometimes when people are distraught, full of hatred and confused, they take it out on their own bodies. When someone does harm to him or herself, we say it is self-destructive; we know it is not healthy. It is pathological to injure the body in which you live...to harm the self *and* believe it is good. That is the essence of any addiction. We know from research that ongoing use of pornography shapes the brain. We know it cripples relationships. We also know that the chronic use of pornography lowers inhibitions in a similar fashion to alcohol. It numbs the self to things that our God hates.

Let's consider the biography of deception in a life. We have said that deception's origin is in the human heart and that none of us are exempt. It is there – you and I know its presence in our own hearts and have heard its whisper. All of us have yielded to it. All of us know the heart experience of temptation and the response of self-deception, seemingly working in concert to convince us of its rightness or harmlessness. When we also have a fear of God in our hearts, then another factor is introduced into this battle in the soul. If there is no fear of God or *we silence that fear*, then we can easily begin thinking what the enemy told Eve – you will not die... it will not hurt you. We convince ourselves we can stop at any time... one more time will not hurt... just one more look. If we engage in such self-delusion long enough, we will, over time, lose our taste for good *and* our power to loathe evil. We eventually silence the voice of God and our response of fear to that voice. The problem, of course, is that sin *will* hurt us; and contrary to what the enemy told Eve, it will lead to death. Once we begin removing our taste for good and our power to hate evil, then we only habituate that which causes our death; or as the psalmist says in Psalm 36:4 (NASB), "He sets himself on a path that is not good." As deception becomes a way of life, evil can be easily practiced by an increasingly dead soul that is presumptuous, planning and actively participating in evil. Over time, the possibility for penitence is destroyed and the habit ends in soul death. It is a sobering and frightening picture.

If we truly see the life-destroying capacity of such addictions, we will not settle for a mere discontinuation of the behavior. We will want to see – in ourselves and our clients – a transformation of longing. Merely repressing the darkness we have pursued is not sufficient. We must, instead, be full of light. Change and holiness are not just restraining old passions (that is simply the beginning) – they are the growth of a new passion that grips the soul more deeply than the former addiction. It is a long, hard road to go from addiction and deceit to habituated love and obedience to our God.

May we, as counselors, come out of the cold that has numbed us, from the painlessness that deceives, and the sin that no longer stings in our own lives. May we stand before the Light of the World, whose scorching light will disturb us, but by whose stripes we will be healed. May our own injections of deception never become comfortable. May we who are His people eagerly look for the God who searches hearts so that out of us will pour, not deceit, but rivers of living water into the parched, deceived souls with whom we work.

For further thought:

Read and meditate on Psalm 36.

> *"Sin takes from a man his healthy taste for what is good and his power to loathe evil, and then deludes him with the idea that he still has both."*
>
> **George Adam Smith[10]**

---

[10] *The Sabbath Recorder,* 1917, Vol. 83, no. 6.

The Spiritual Cancer Within

Theologians have often taught that in the Scriptures leprosy is a metaphor depicting sin. It is a picture in the physical realm of the disease of sin in the spiritual realm. With leprosy, there is often an extended period of several years between infection and the appearance of symptoms. It causes nerve damage and the victim's warning signals of danger to the body are rendered useless. One of the results can be an erosion of the body; it literally gets eaten away by unnoticed damage. Leprosy results in weakness and often leads to blindness. The similarities to sin are easy to see. One can engage in sinful practice internally or privately without outward symptoms for a long time. Sin deadens the conscience toward God and the warning signals of the Spirit are rendered useless. The life of God in the individual is eroded and certainly results in moral weakness and spiritual blindness. This is an apt analogy worthy of consideration.

In recent years, I have watched quite a few people I know and love be stricken with cancer. Christopher

Hitchens, an author and well-known atheist, wrote about his diagnosis of esophageal cancer on the *Vanity Fair* blog[11]. He talks about selling his memoir, *Hitch-22*, one day and throwing up backstage the next; crossing the line from what he believed was healthy "into the land of malady." The physicians he saw showed him "postcards from the interior" and then told him he needed an oncologist. Does that sound familiar to you as a counselor? Someone comes to you with various outward symptoms that he or she thinks are fixable and, after an "examination," you realize the internal destruction is quite serious. Like Hitchens, that person continues in denial for weeks or months, perhaps even years, while attempting to live as if everything is fine. Yet, relentlessly, the symptoms continue and even increase until at some point he or she can no longer deny the pain and damage that is occurring.

Hitchens says he discovered that his cancer had spread when the physician palpated his clavicle where the cancer was big enough to be seen and felt. How like sin, which lies below the surface and is practiced privately or behind closed doors until one day it can be seen by others. He tells us that though it could be seen, the doctors did not yet know the primary source. "Carcinoma works cunningly from the inside out. Detection and treatment often work more slowly and gropingly from the outside in." Think of the client who comes to

---

[11] Christopher Hitchens, "Topic of Cancer," *Vanity Fair,* last modified August, 2010,
https://www.vanityfair.com/culture/2010/09/hitchens-201009

you because of immorality (the cancer can be seen). Very often, people have no idea how they got to such a place. And so begins the slow process of detection and treatment for whatever is buried, tucked inside, away from the light and breeding, sending out tentacles of sin. Working back from the things that are known, we seek to see and understand the original site of disease and follow the metastases so that our interventions can be comprehensive, and any recurrence of the disease is prohibited.

Christopher Hitchens poignantly states that his father had also died of esophageal cancer and, speaking of himself that "in whatever kind of a 'race' life may be, he too had very abruptly become a finalist." As Christians, we know the race that is set before us. We also know we are all finalists. Hopefully, we are keenly aware of the fact that we, too, carry within us the very disease of sin that always brings forth death.

The cancer of sin in a leader has tremendous ramifications, for the tentacles spread not only throughout the leader's life, but also throughout the lives of those who follow. The body of the Church is organic. We impact one another. When we hide away our sinful thoughts and choices so we can keep them, nurture them, and feed off them, we deaden ourselves to the voice of the Spirit of God. This dynamic in a leader will eventually bear the fruit of death: immorality, idolatry, strife, jealousy, division, envy... (Galatians 5:20-21 NIV). Hidden sin *will* eventually metastasize; it *will* extend tentacles that reach out through a life, a family, a ministry, and even a nation.

May we fear sin in our souls and protect against it with the fierceness we would use to avoid cancer in our bodies. May we be "steadfast (personally faithful), immovable (not swayed by adversaries), always abounding (running over) in the work of the Lord" (1 Corinthians 15:58 (NASB), "to the end that we who were the first to hope in Christ should be to the praise of His glory" (Ephesians 1:12 NASB).

For further thought:

How have you seen the cancer of sin manifest itself? Pray for the wisdom to unearth deception and the courage to recognize and treat the metastasis.

> *"Be no mere spectator, turn the glass round upon yourself and see how much it signifies, both that you are a sinner and a man. All that you see without, in the wars, revenges and crazed religions of the world is faithfully represented in the appalling disorders of your own spirit."*
>
> **Horace Bushnell**[12]

---

[12] Horace Bushnell, *Sermons for the New Life* (New York, NY: Charles Scribner's Sons, 1876), 69.

To Heal or To Hide

A system consists of things or people so closely con-
nected as to make an organic whole. The concept of
wholeness implies that a system has power significantly greater than any one of its individual parts. All
that power is brought to bear when the system is threatened. That is a good and often lifesaving response when
a system is threatened by disease or injury. It is life en-
dangering when that force is used to hide something
that is not right.

Think of the system of the physical body as an example. If I experience pain in one of my eyes, it gets immediate attention. It waters automatically. I close it and my
other eye takes over seeing for me. My hands help by
getting water to flush it out. My brain processes what is
happening and makes the decision of whether to call an
ophthalmologist. Something is wrong and the system
unites all its power to get it made right and protect the
injured part in a way that is healing and restorative.

Conversely, suppose I find a lump on my body and decide to ignore it. I am fearful of what it might mean; I do not want to go through all the appointments and tests and possible treatment that could be required. I know if it is cancerous, the treatment is likely to make me sick or even cause more damage to my body. So, I choose to conceal it and even attempt to "hide" it from myself. You might tell me my response is foolish and that my efforts at denial could cost me my health or my life.

You would, of course, be correct, but systems of many kinds often hide signs of potential illness. Families of addicts do this with regularity, as do families with incest. The system uses its power to such an extent that the victim knows not to speak and even works very hard to present a healthy face to the world. Many of you work with sick systems that revolve around addiction, sexual abuse, or domestic violence. You, too, have felt the power that rears its head when anyone tries to drag the truth to the light and names the real problem and asks for help. An entire family will deny the truth and alienate a victim or truthteller rather than face the fact that there is a cancerous lump that is metastasizing and destroying the system.

We also know that this occurs with regularity in much larger systems – systems that bear the name of Christ. We have seen it in the Church, in missions and in Christian organizations around the world. There is the cancer of immorality, theft, corruption, or sexual abuse... and all the energy of that system goes to maintaining itself and a good appearance while ignoring the disease. Thinking they are preserving the "work" – called God's work – they fail to see and deal with the disease hidden within. It is, however, no step toward the recovery of a sickly system to disguise the worst symptoms of that system to itself.

We say it is the work of the Lord and that we are using the power of the system to protect the work. The Israelites used to say, "The temple of Jehovah," while they were worshipping idols, and God's response was a call to righteousness. He called them to make their ways and doings healthy and not to tolerate sin in their midst – no matter what they called their actions. No system – family, church, or institution – is God's work unless it is full of truth and love. Toleration of sin, pretense, disease, crookedness, or deviation from the truth means the system is *not* the work of God.

Some of us have faced the power of systems that name God's name, yet look nothing like him. That power can be formidable. It is hard to fight an organic whole, particularly when that system is full of people you love or those important to you and your future. We have seen in bold letters the power of such systems such as Nazi Germany, Rwanda, and Bosnia. They seem to easily sweep others along into participation in their corrupt ways. How much easier it is to keep quiet or be swept along, especially when the system has been about good work done in the name of God. We forget that anything done in the name of God that does not bear His character throughout is in reality not of Him at all.

God thought up systems. He created family; the people of Israel; the Church He intends for them to be vibrant and full of the health of likeness to him. They are to bless this world and be a force for righteousness among men. When they are not, his people who are called by his name are to humble themselves and seek his face and give the call to repentance and righteousness that he might be truly glorified in His work.

For further thought:

Meditate on the quote below and how it relates to the use of power in systems. How can the Church become a sanctuary that does not protect sin?

> *"His mercy is a holy mercy which knows how to pardon sin, not to protect it; it is a sanctuary for the penitent, not for the presumptuous."*
>
> **Bishop Reynolds**[13]

---

[13] *The Churchman's Monthly Magazine*, 1859, Vol. 6, no. 4.

The Parable of Rwanda

When our God was here in the flesh, one of the things He did was teach through parables. He used the method of story or verbal pictures to invite humans with hard hearts and blind eyes to look again. Jesus longed for people to answer the invitation in the picture.

I am not certain why it took me so long, but somewhere along the way I realized that parables are God's perpetual method. He has never ceased to use pictures to woo slow, blind sheep. There have been many such images in my work and travels by which I have been lured into the heart of our God. Rwanda is one of those.

I returned to Rwanda for my sixth trip, along with six colleagues – a long-term dream that came to fruition. We were there to teach trainers at a three-day conference, building on the foundation of previous trainings. You may recall that Rwanda was the place of a 100-day genocide in 1994, where nearly one million people were slaughtered with machetes and nail-studded clubs. The killing was done in schools, homes, churches, along the roads, and anywhere else you can imagine. It took place at the hands of neighbors, friends, and fellow church members. People ran into churches hoping for sanctuary and were killed inside by the thousands – ten in one, 15,000 in another, and so on.

It has been many years since those tragedies occurred while the world watched and did nothing. Needless to say, Rwanda is a traumatized country. It also has very few citizens with any academic or professional counselor training, and those who have some level of training are genocide victims themselves, some having lost 40, 60, and in one case, 102 family members to the machete. We go to train and bring resources – books, videos, and publications – and are privileged to know them, hear their stories, and strengthen their good work. These counselors are the frontline caregivers for others who have been profoundly traumatized. So, how is such a country – physically stunning, but carrying the wounds of brutality – a parable?

Many visited Rwanda years ago before the genocide, saw its stunning beauty and thousand green hills, and called it Eden. That Eden was destroyed by people – as all Edens are. People like us, who divided the world into "us" and "them." People called those deemed "them," names. In Rwanda, "they" were cockroaches. Individuals nursed resentments about "them" – killing another in their hearts. That hatred was fed politically, economically, and ethnically... even by teachers, pastors, and priests. It is not a big jump, then, for someone to say, "If we get rid of the cockroaches, we will all be better off.

It will be good for us and good for Rwanda." That is exactly what they did – they exterminated their own citizens whom they no longer saw as people created in the image of God but, rather, as insects infecting the land. The scope and intimacy of the brutality lead us to think that atrocities, such as killing one's neighbors or students or parishioners, are far removed from us.

Pause now... look at the picture with me – the picture I have seen, studied, and heard for several years. Have we ever divided the world of humans created in the image of God into them and us? I think the answer is "yes." We do it to each other... to fellow church members. It occurs between parents and children and between spouses. "They" are wrong, or stupid or bad or less than – cockroaches – and we justify slaughtering them with our thoughts and words. We even use spiritual things to do so – oh, we do not use iron crosses from altars like the Rwandans did – we use Scripture verses or doctrine to chop instead.

I have come to love Rwanda. It is a privilege to teach and train fellow believers and caregivers, and to learn from them as well. It is also a painful place. Genocide, rape, and orphan stories are hard to bear. Nevertheless, Rwanda has taught me several precious lessons through many wonderful people – eternal lessons that are changing me. This is one of them – look at the parable and answer its invitation to see:

• Sin is a frightful, deforming, corrupting poison and so-called little resentments, little criticisms, and little acts of impurity carry in them the tsunami of genocide and death. We think they are little, that no one is really hurt by them. God says sin leads to death. Yet we do not think of our own transgressions the way he does. God would have us see the picture and not be deceived. He says the little sins with which we are comfortable carry the same poison that was in the hearts of those who swung machetes and iron crosses in Rwanda.

- God himself is the ultimate parable – the Word made flesh – made into a living picture. And that parable, like Rwanda, makes clear that his response to a groaning creation, a corrupted Eden – both in our hearts and all around us – is a call to us as His body to sit down, dwell among those who groan, and look like him in that place. You see, Rwanda has taught me that there is no "them," only us – cockroaches every last one of us. However, although we are cockroaches, we are still loved and pursued by our God who perpetually gives us pictures so we might see Him and then be like Him, offering, as He did, a picture in the flesh in this world – His world – that He so loves.

For further thought:

Reflect on this parable of Rwanda. What stands out to you?

> *"I am but a stranger in this world, wherever I may be situated, or however I may happen to be distinguished. And surely it is my privilege that I am so. When I look not upon myself as a stranger and a pilgrim, when I am captivated in this place of my exile, I forget myself, and act far beneath my character as a candidate for an immortal crown."*
>
> ***John Fawcett***[14]

---

[14] John Fawcett, *Miscellanea Sacra or, The Theological Miscellany: Volume 1* (Halifax: Ewood Hall, 1799), 225.

DAY 13

Brief Meditation 3

"Many go very far in a profession of religion, and yet live in the habitual indulgence of some sin, either great or small, secret or open. Judas made so fair a show, that all the other disciples questioned their own sincerity rather than his."

John Fawcett[15]

---

[15] John Fawcett, *Christ Precious to Those Who Believe: A Practical Treatise on Faith and Love* (London: William Milner, 1839), 99.

DAY 14

Brief Meditation 4

"Leaders, laboring for their righteous
hopes, whose private lives have been
unworthy, and the success of such men
with their apparent indispensableness
for the moment to some high cause of
reform, have led to the conclusion that
private character is of no importance."

George Adam Smith[16]

---

[16] George Adam Smith, *The Expositor's Bible: The Book of
Isaiah Volumes I and II* (London: Hodder and Stoughton Publishers, 1890).

Week 3

The Weak Strengthen the Strong

In 1 Corinthians 12, Paul goes on to say the following: "Those parts of the body that seem to be weaker are indispensable, and the parts that we think are less honorable we treat with special honor. And the parts that are unpresentable are treated with special modesty, while our presentable parts need no special treatment" (vv. 22-24 NIV).

What happens to you when you are around weak, sick, odd, or unattractive people? We often see the weak as a hindrance, don't we? We respond that way to our own weakness. It gets in the way. It slows things down. If you walk with someone who is weaker than you are, you cannot walk as fast as you normally would. If you talk with someone who thinks more slowly than you do, you must restrain yourself.

What do we do with things we consider less honorable? The term simply means less valuable, less worthy. We make time for what we value and what we deem of little value gets ignored or pushed aside. Is it not the same with people? Those we consider worthy, we talk to, spend time with, and wait for. Those we see as less valuable get little to nothing from us.

What do we do if we decide something is unpresentable? If you have a room in your house that you believe is not fit to be exhibited, when someone stops by, you shut the door. To have someone see us with someone who is not presentable tends to humiliate us and lead us to quickly explain ourselves.

God says some utterly amazing things about how you and I are to be with the weak, the less honorable, and the less presentable. He says that the parts of the body that are weaker are, in fact, necessary! Something that is necessary is something we cannot get along without. How can that which is weaker be necessary? Let me show you something I learned a few years ago.

If I live either separate from other people, or only with those who are just like me, I will find it very easy to live in deception because there will be nothing to clash against me. If who I am is not really in agreement with my image of myself, I will tend to exclude myself from those situations or people that bring home to me the reality of who I am. For example, I believe that those who know Christ are to be patient with others. I believe I am a patient person. It will be easy for me to hold that belief as long as I am not with those who are slower or who do not get it or cannot do it. Put me in relationship with someone for whom I must wait, and we will see if I am indeed a patient person. Those in the body who are weaker are necessary because God uses them to expose our self-deceptions. They are some of God's teachers to his people.

We tend to push the weaker to get stronger and so bankrupt ourselves. If instead I will bow with humility, God will use what I by nature despise to teach me about myself and to drive me to him. And we think when we see those who are weaker that they just need us! How arrogant and how unlike God who used the weak things of this world – mangers, babies, towels, and crosses – to serve as a backdrop highlighting who he really is. The weak things of this world merely exposed his longsuffering, his beauty, and his great love. They revealed his glory.

God also says that the parts of the body we deem less honorable are those we are to treat with special honor. Typically, the more honorable someone is in our estimation, the more honor we accord him or her. Someone famous gets more attention; someone unknown gets little to nothing.

You and I are part of the kingdom of God rather than the kingdom of this world. To accord honor to the little, the insignificant, and the devalued is to live as a child of God. He is no respecter of persons. The presence of the less honorable among us afford us the opportunity to demonstrate that we are children of God's kingdom, rather than the kingdom of this world.

Finally, God says the parts that are less presentable are to be treated with special modesty. To say that something is not presentable is to say that it is unfit, inappropriate, or unattractive in some way. We hide what is unpresentable. What happens when we spill something on our clothes? We try to hide it. We want people we think are not presentable to be quiet, to go away, or to not disturb.

Scripture does not call us to hide them, nor does it call us to parade them. We are to treat them appropriately, suitably, giving them what they have not received or do not know how to do. To treat another with special modesty is to treat them with suitability. In other words, teach them by your behavior what presentability looks like.

To live in the body of Christ as God has called us to, is to live out values radically different from the values of this world. It means walking in great humility, according honor where it is generally not given, all the while bending to the work of God's Spirit in our lives as those we deem less important are used by God to expose us to ourselves. Anyone God uses to teach us more of Christ and conform us to his image is a gift indeed!

For further thought:

What are some things you have learned from the people who are considered "weak" in this world? Pray for humility as God continues to teach us more about himself through what may make us uncomfortable.

> *"He employs for his purpose the unlikeliest means and agencies. He makes the ravenous birds have their instincts in abeyance in order that they may minister to his servant...those who feed on rotting cadavers become servant birds of supply."*
>
> **John Macduff**[17]

---

[17] John Ross Macduff, *The Prophet of Fire: Or, the Life and times of Elijah* (London: James Nisbet & Co., 1864), 42.

Feeding the Hungry

R wanda – land of a thousand hills; tropical beauty; gracious, welcoming people. Rwanda – land of a brutal genocide; one million dead in 100 days; suffering, traumatized people. I spent a week there with a professional ministry team listening, questioning, observing, and dialoguing. We heard from government officials, medical personnel, educators, pastors, lay counselors, genocide perpetrators, and genocide survivors. They were united in their comments to us.

A universal theme heard again and again was "we are coming out of a coma." It has been years since the genocide, but much of that time has been spent on basic survival needs and the building of an infrastructure. Many are still without running water and electricity. Medical care is very limited. Unemployment is high, as is illiteracy. The entire culture has been permeated with a genocidal ideology. Most believed that if societal and government structures were developed, then traumatic stress responses would ease or disappear. Yet, after all these years, the incidence and awareness of post-traumatic stress disorder continues to increase at an alarming rate. Many are now realizing that in a broader sense, the whole of Rwandan society is deeply traumatized.

While all the survivors are obviously traumatized, I found the same to be true with many of the perpetrators, both the imprisoned and the released. Countless thousands who fled the country, as well as those who have survived in refugee camps, have PTSD. There are a great number of widows who not only lost husbands and children to the genocide, but who were also raped and contracted HIV-AIDS, having to now raise the children born as the result of those violent assaults. Trauma is also rampant among those of the younger generations. There are children whose parents were killed, those who are the result of rape, those whose parents have HIV-AIDS, those whose parents died while fleeing the country, those whose parents are in prison as perpetrators, and multitudes of children who are simply traumatized "by what they see in their culture."

As Rwanda is "coming out of this coma" and seeing the level of trauma across the entire country, they are also pleading for help. From the highest levels of government to the most basic of caregiving, we heard the same request: "Please come. When can you start? We are desperate."

Samuel Rutherford, a prominent Presbyterian author and theologian, once said, "Our best fare here is hunger."[18] Human beings do not like hunger, need, or unmet longings... still less do we like desperation. We want satisfaction, to be full, and a determined will does almost anything to ensure that we have it. We steal; we lie; we commit adultery; we manipulate; and we use illicit, sinful things to satiate our hunger. However, hunger can also make us more receptive and create a willing heart to receive from others, which makes us very vulnerable, for if the hunger is strong enough, we could end up ingesting any substance at all, even that which might destroy or kill.

As counselors, we often see the above dynamic in chronically abused children who are starving for love and a nurturing relationship from their adult caregivers. They will, in their desperation, even go to the one who abuses them just to receive some kind of meaningful touch. Sadly, the abuser only uses the child's hunger to feed himself. Rwanda is starving in much the same way. Rwanda is also vulnerable. In her hunger, she has opened her heart and mind to receive counseling that is Christian, and faith based. However, in her vulnerability, she is easy prey for those who would use her for their own sordid gain.

In thinking about this, I have been struck by James 1:27 (NASB) which says, "pure and undefiled religion in the sight of our God and Father is this: to visit orphans and widows in their distress, and *to keep oneself unstained by the world* [emphasis mine]." Our God is

---

[18] Samuel Rutherford, *Christ and His Cross* (New York, NY: Longmans, Green, & Co., 1902), 77.

calling us as His church to go, to see, and to relieve the anguish of the widows and orphans. The Church has an astounding and rare opportunity here to come alongside the needy and vulnerable, the traumatized victims and perpetrators of genocide, with the tools and resources of Christian counseling that are rooted in the love of Christ and His Word.

The call, however, is accompanied with a warning. We are to do so while remaining unsoiled by the world. We will be unsafe for the people of Rwanda and our own clients unless we have allowed our hungers to drive us to the eternal Fountain of Life. Wherever we satisfy our own hungers with those things of an inferior nature, we become unsafe for the needy and vulnerable of this world; for in that moment, we run the risk of using them for our own "food." John Fawcett, a writer and disciple of George Whitfield, said, "When I look not upon myself as a stranger and a pilgrim, when I am captivated with anything in this place of my exile, I forget myself and act far beneath my character, as a candidate for an immortal crown."[19] Rwanda is certainly a call to the Church to help. Rwanda is also a call to the body of Christ to pursue him *before* all other pursuits.

---

[19] John Fawcett, *Christ Precious to Those Who Believe*, excerpted, Grace Gems, https://gracegems.org/28/fawcett_christ_precious3.htm (accessed 26 July 2019), Part 2, ch.3, section 4, para. 27.

For further thought:

What do you hunger for? How do you respond to your hunger?

> *"If a nation or man is religious in its deepest life but not also in the activities of that life, it is persisting in disobedience to an inward conviction and presently that conviction will no longer appeal...but will become a solace which is false – a refuge which is a refuge of lies."*
>
> **G. Campbell Morgan**[20]

---

[20] G. Campbell Morgan, *Studies in the Prophecy of Jeremiah*, 57. Used with permission; see References.

The Human Will

It is striking to me how rarely we, as counselors, talk about the will. We talk about behavior, emotion, and cognition... we talk about history, memory, and relationship, but we do not talk about the human will. It is there; we encounter it in every therapeutic dialogue. We often meet it in its resistant, obstructionist form.

Human will was there from the beginning – "from *any* tree you may eat freely" (i.e., choose as you will). However, "from the tree of the knowledge of good and evil you *shall not eat*" (i.e., exercise your will against this). We did not listen, and human will has, since that fateful day, bent us away from God.

We see the outcome of that bending as we work with our clients. The shaping of a child's malleable will in the context of abuse has disastrous effects. It is bent toward helplessness, retreat, and self-protection. Or perhaps it is bent toward rage and destruction of others. In some, we see both outcomes simultaneously. In those who grow up without loving discipline, we see a bending toward impulsivity, chaos, and the service of self. For others, the exercise of the will seemed useless and so its power is now exercised only to refuse, obstruct, or resist.

It is vital that counselors understand the bend of a client's will so as to work with them effectively. Simply coming up against another's will head-on or attempting to face another with our verbal or emotional power will yield little in terms of productive outcome. God's way of working with our wills, which are so bent against him, is instructive. He does not force, but rather pursues with grace, invites, or, when necessary, allows us to have what we will and then graciously uses the consequences of our choices to turn us back to Him. The father in the parable of Luke 15 permitted the son to have what he willed. The natural outcome of the son's choice was that he became lower than the swine he tended. That outcome brought the son to his senses and led to a new bending of his will – "I *will* arise and go to my father."

Another aspect of the will that is vital for us as counselors to understand is that repeated bowing yields slavery. In other words, the things we practice submitting to eventually own us. The Apostle Paul says that when we will ourselves over to something or someone, we become its slave (Romans 6:16 NIV). This is readily apparent when considering things like cocaine or alcohol. It is less obvious when considering attitudes, thoughts, and prejudices. George Adam Smith, a 19th century Scottish theologian, said this, "The habituated flesh becomes the suggester of crime to the will which first constrained it to sin, and now wearily *but in vain* rebels against the habits of its instrument."[21] Repeated submission eventually results in an inability to stop.

For further thought:

How has God used the things you desired to teach you more about who He is? Is there anything that is keeping you from Him? What is your heart bent towards?

"There are no forces or facts upon which God does not lay His hand in quiet strength and majesty and make them tributary to the accomplishment of His purpose."

G. Campbell Morgan[22]

---

[21] George Adam Smith, *The Expositor's Bible: The Book of Isaiah Volumes I and II* (London: Hodder and Stoughton Publishers, 1890), 152.

[22] G. Campbell Morgan, *Exposition of the Whole Bible: Chapter by Chapter in One Volume* (Grand Rapids, MI: Fleming H. Revell, Co., 1959), 29. Used with permission; see References.

And a Little Child Leads Them

Parenting can be an adventure full of exquisite joy and run the gamut all the way to fear, grief, and great sorrow. I do not think we realize the great vulnerability parenting brings on us until our children arrive. The impact of such tiny lives is quite profound. It also never goes away no matter how big they get or how far away they end up. We are impacted by their love, joys, successes, and accomplishments. We are equally susceptible to their hurts, sorrows, limitations, and failures. The only protection from such vulnerabilities is the hardness of the heart for a failure to love.

Our vulnerability and the resulting effect of our children's lives lead to something few ever mention – a core principle that I believe is one of the integral parts of parenting. We meet these tiny people and feel overwhelmed at all that is required of us. Their basic care

rests on our shoulders as they can do nothing for themselves. We must teach and train and shape these little
lives. They are stunningly vulnerable, and most adults
have some sense of how easily we could hurt them. We
want them to grow up strong and healthy and wise. We
may feel utterly inadequate for the task and are keenly
aware of all they will require from milk to education to
ethical and spiritual training. We are to be there for
them. What is less readily seen, however, is that they
are also there for us. We are their training ground and
they are ours. We shape them; they shape us. Both sides
actually go to "school" simultaneously.

Many years ago, when my firstborn was still quite
small, he did something naughty (I no longer remember
what it was) that required a time out. I was about six
months pregnant. I took him by the hand and led him
upstairs to the chair we used. He cried for a bit and then
I came in and spoke with him and we went back down
to the dinner table. He did it again... and again. On my
third or so trip down the stairs, I sat down on the land-
ing and said out loud to myself, "Who in the world is actually getting disciplined here?" The light went on. I
suddenly realized I was being trained by my Heavenly
Father just as much as my son was being trained by his
earthly mother. He was learning to obey his mommy. I
was learning to teach him over and over with patience
and a gentle, but firm, voice (not my natural inclination). If I chose not to bow to the training of my Father,
then the training of my son would be out of balance. My
son, with all his gifts and precious ways... as well as his
struggles, had been sent to me for parenting, teaching

and loving. He had also been sent to me so I might learn more of the ways of my Father in heaven and be shaped more into His likeness. How like God to take what we quickly see as a one-way street and make it into a two-way experience! The revelation changed the dialogue in my head from thinking, "What does my son need to do or learn or be?" to "Father, how would You have me respond? What is the best for my son from Your perspective?" Fortunately, for both of my sons, it made a significant difference in the responses of their mother over the years.

Such thinking is quite unlike our natural responses. We get angry because of what our children did or did not do; we are impatient when they do not/will not learn; we discipline out of our own emotions rather than out of the nature of Christ, and we forget their littleness, their limitations, and vulnerability. We want them to do the right thing, the convenient thing, mostly because it will make our lives easier or smoother. We are self-serving in that way, rather than being a servant.

Therapy is, of course, quite similar. Broken, hurting, angry, thrashing, vulnerable people come to us for counseling. We are to be there for them. We are to reflect, empathize, suggest, question, and teach so that they might learn and grow and find comfort. Yet once again, our Father is after us and uses their anger, repetitive behaviors or failures, anxiety, irrationality, and deep wounds, to call us to bow so that He might shape us into His image no matter what gets thrown at us. Both parenting and therapy invite us to learn the ways of our incarnational God, who put on human flesh and showed us how to walk in love and truth – not only influencing and shaping those around us, but also by being shaped so that in our flesh we carry the fragrance and likeness of Christ into those relationships.

For further thought:

Think about the moments that have frustrated, angered, or irritated you. What could God be teaching you through those moments? How is He shaping you through the people He has put you in relationship with?

"He is the greatest of victors who knows that God is on the field when he is most invisible. Circumstances of difficulty are opportunities for faith, and the measure of our perplexity in service and in the Christian life is the measure of our opportunity."

G. Campbell Morgan[23]

---

[23] G. Campbell Morgan, *The Acts of the Apostles* (Grand Rapids, MI: Fleming H. Revell, Co., 1934), 376-377. Used with permission; see References.

Intimacy With God

Picture a stage, and in the back of the stage is a curtain along its length. Behind the curtain is God. He has called you, as his child, to leave your life on the stage and come behind the curtain to find him and know him. He desires for you to grasp what it means to be full of his life – the life which makes all things alive again. He asks you to kneel with Him in Gethsemane and enter into His suffering; to follow Him to the cross and learn what it means to be conformed to His death. He fills you full with his own life and then returns you to the stage. You enter back into your life on this planet.

The stage is a metaphor of the life you have now with all its varied circumstances. And on that stage, full of other people, for the rest of your life, he wants you to live. Sometimes, the stage can be confusing, chaotic, hurtful, lonely, pressured, too crowded, or dark. It is the place where you live out the life you found with God and will continue to find in him whenever you're behind the curtain. Your life on the stage is to make sense *based on, and because of, your life with God behind the curtain* – not based on what is seen on the stage. Everything you do on the stage – every reaction, every thought, every choice, and every word – is to make sense based on the life behind the life... the life hidden with Christ in God. It is our relationship with Him that gives life to our involvement on this stage we call earth.

As counselors, we know that the stage of life is a mess in many ways. We also know we are called to impact the conditions found on that stage. We *are* to "do justice and love mercy." We *are* to reach out with compassion and sacrificially serve the poor, the imprisoned, and the brokenhearted on this stage. We are called to be so full of the life of God that it spills out all over the stage as we move around and interact with others. However, you and I cannot *fix* the stage. I think that as Christians, we often forget that it is the life of Christ *in* us that impacts the stage, and we get focused on merely trying to rearrange the mess that is already there.

Now I truly understand that where we stand on the stage, who is around us, and what the props are matters. The placements and props on the stage have profound implications. They are not insignificant. Those of you who have worked with sexual abuse, violence in the home, depression, or chronic illness know how desperately significant the surroundings on the stage can be. As Christians, we are often called to move people around, help them find new lines, and alter the props that surround them – but we are not to be controlled by the stage. The stage, with all its accoutrements and their

importance, *is not central*. The stage, for all its significance and power, is not to be the thing that *governs us*.

We are to live on the stage governed by the life behind the life. We are to live governed by the God in
whom we live and move and have our being. We are to
live on this stage with our lives hidden with Christ in
God. We are not to be ruled by the stage, the earthly di-
rectors, the players, the props, or the script. Do you
glimpse a sense of the massive pressure that surrounds
us to conform to anything but the life behind the life?

A close look at the life of Mary, the sister of Lazarus,
gives us a good picture of what it looks like to live on
the stage when the governing relationship is the one
with Christ. We have in Mary a woman who broke with
tradition, who refused to let the accepted place for
women keep her from studying at the feet of her master. Her pursuit of Jesus far outweighed the traditions,
expectations, and roles of her culture – things which
pressure all of us. We have in Mary a woman who
looked at the realities of life in this world and grieved.
She knew full well what the loss of her brother meant
for her. She had lost her brother, her place, and her security. She did not allow the weight of that loss to em-
bitter or harden her. She allowed it to drive her to the
feet of Jesus, who wept with her and miraculously
brought glory to God in a place of death. We have in
Mary a woman so consumed with love for Jesus that
nothing was allowed to prevent her expression of that
love. She poured out her security for the future on His
feet, again breaking with tradition, even weathering the
criticism of His followers.

A study of her life will help us see how Mary's relationship with, and love for, Jesus overrode all else in her world. She sought him out; she studied him; she listened to him; she learned of him; and she came to some understanding of him and who he was. Then she went on to conduct her life based on that relationship. It drove her and governed her; it had mastered her. If you want to grasp what ruled Mary on the stage of life, you do not need to look at the script, or the props, or even the other players. You need to know and understand the life behind her life. Mary only makes sense in the context of Jesus. If you would understand her, you must know something of him. She lived hidden with Christ in God. She lived and moved and had her being in Jesus Christ. And then she lived *out of that vibrant life* in the midst of her circumstances.

In Isaiah 11, where the Messiah is described, it says this: "He will not judge by what His eyes see, nor make a decision by what His ears hear but with righteousness" (vv. 3-4 NASB). We are basically being told here that Jesus functioned in life not based on what was seen or heard on the stage, but according to the character of God. What is good, right, and true was determined by who God is, *not by the information gleaned on the stage*. On the stage it may feel loving to tolerate sin, but behind the curtain is One who hates sin. On the stage it may seem right to make harsh judgments, but behind the curtain is One who pours out grace and mercy. On the stage it may be very frightening, but behind the curtain sits the faithful One, the Rock. Isaiah says that Jesus only makes sense in light of understanding the Father and His character.

That is our call. To live so riveted on the Master, ruled by love of him, living obedient to him, explainable to others *only* by understanding him. We are to live so that when others see us, they see the One who sent us. See me – and you will see the life behind my life. That is the call. Where is the power for such a life? It lies behind the curtain. It is found in the One who is himself the resurrection and the life. On what are our eyes riveted? What has surpassing value for us? What script are we following? What governs our lives? When someone looks at our lives on the stage, do they see Him? Do we make sense to others only in light of Jesus Christ?

For further thought:

Take some time to reflect on the questions written in the last paragraph.

> "When the kingdom of God is set up within you, the outer life shapes itself to the new purpose and aim. The writ and will of the King run through every department, even to its outmost frontier while thoughts, feelings and desires and all the coinage of the heart bear, not as before the image of the self, but rather the image and superscription of the Invisible King."
>
> **Henry Burton**[24]

---

[24] Henry Burton, *The Expositor's Bible: The Gospel According to Luke*, 253-254.

Brief Meditation 5

"Those who do not make the precepts of Christ the rule of their lives, are to be looked upon as no Christians, let them say ever such fine things of His law."

Justin Martyr[25]

---

[25] *The Apologies of Justin Martyr, Tertullian, and Minutius Felix in Defence of the Christian Religion, 1709, Vol. 1.*

Brief Meditation 6

"The fact that something is common
does not redeem it from its ugliness."

G. Campbell. Morgan[26]

---

[26] G. Campbell Morgan, *The Great Physician: A Series of Fifty Studies, the Method of Jesus with Individuals* (Grand Rapids, MI: Fleming H. Revell, Co., 1937), 219. Used with permission; see References.

Week 4

Our Composer and Our Marriages

As one who has been in the counseling profession for more than four decades, I am often reminded of one of the great hazards of that profession. Anyone who does the work of counseling full time runs the risk of becoming so focused on the lives of other people that his or her own gets swallowed up. The energy required to listen attentively, handle crises, and manage the complex dynamics of other marriages can easily result in little or no energy being directed toward one's own personal life. One of the areas that is often neglected is the marriage of the counselor.

Neglect of one's own marriage is very easy to fall into. Long hours and the outpouring of tremendous relational energy mean that a very tired human being goes home at the end of the day – one who has no inclination to talk or listen to another member of the human race.

It is very easy to expect a spouse to grasp the intensity and importance of what you have done all day and, in response, be perfectly willing to put his or her own needs on hold. We are, after all, very busily, altruistically, and sacrificially helping other people! Being a relatively normal member of the race, and a therapist by trade, I have not found myself exempt from such struggles during my 40 plus years of marriage.

It has produced a conflict for me, however. I have lodged somewhere in my brain and my heart the very strong belief that our God has called us to be what we teach. Such a belief often makes life complicated because it requires seemingly constant wrestling with those myriad influences which would delude us into thinking that some inconsistency or slipshod living tucked away in a corner will not hurt anybody. I believe God has said otherwise. That belief requires me to sit down with some regularity and consider my life, my choices, my attitudes, and my relationships in the light of the Word of God. My marriage is not exempt from such assessment.

I find, when assessing anything, whether it is in my own life or a client's life, that it is important not to get stuck using the same language all the time. If I do not continually stretch my mind and look for new categories, I find I get into a rut, the assessment becomes a rote exercise and I miss significant things. Marital assessment is no exception.

It is important to remind us all that there is a governing principle that is foundational to all of life. Our real work in life is not our marriage; it is not counseling; it is not parenting or anything else that competes for our time and attention. Our real work as believers is maintaining our relationship to Jesus Christ above all else. All other arenas of our lives are to be under the dominance of this passion. Paul says in 2 Corinthians 5:9 (NIV), "...we make it our goal to please him." We are not to live our lives ruled by any other ambition. The work of counseling is a good work. It is not our first work. The work of marriage is a good work. It is not our first work. The first work of Jesus Christ was obedience to the Father. Ours is the same. That means the heart of marriage is not about pleasing myself in the relationship, nor is it about pleasing my spouse. The heart of marriage is about living there pleasing to God, wrestling before him over a lifetime to become in that place what he has called me to be.

In marriage we have two people, two voices. Each of these voices is saying something different. Each of these voices is certain that it speaks the truth, that its voice needs to be the dominant one, the one that is heeded. The art of marriage lies in learning how to listen to each of the voices and then bring the two together in a harmonious whole where neither is lost due to the emphasis, intensity, or power of the other.

I have found it helpful to think of marriage as two voices coming together in a harmonious whole, illustrating this concept by means of a music lesson. Johann Sebastian Bach, who happens to be one of my favorite composers, wrote a series of compositions called Two-Part Inventions. The musical concepts behind these marvelous inventions offer an excellent illustration, not only of marriage, but also of the scriptural concept of two made one.

Ephesians 2 was written by Paul regarding the hostilities between Jew and Gentile. However, I think because of Paul's own words in Galatians 3:28 (NIV), we can use this Scripture for the walls that exist sometimes between male and female. Paul said, "There is neither Jew nor Greek, slave nor free, male nor female, for you are all one in Christ Jesus." In other words, those seemingly natural barriers between human beings have, through the cross, been put to death. In the genius of Bach, we find a helpful illustration of the harmony and two distinct voices blended together into a work of beauty.

In order to grasp the concept of two voices that are distinct yet harmonious, we must first be clear about the fact that the "song" of marriage has a Creator/Composer. Marriage is not something men and women thought of themselves. Marriage does not exist because we want sex. It does not exist because we want children. It does not exist because we want companionship. Those are certainly things that push people into marriage, but marriage was originally thought of by God Himself. He is its Creator/Composer.

The book of Genesis tells us, "Then God said, 'Let us make man in our image'... So God created man in his own image...male and female he created them." God said, "Let us create..." And he did. "The Lord God formed the man...and the Lord God made a woman... [and] brought her to the man...and the two became one flesh" (Genesis 1:26-27; 2:7, 22, 24 NIV).

In creating marriage, God gave it two voices: male and female. This duet is part of the image of God. "Let us..." One of the ways we reflect the image of God is differentiation within unity, two voices in one harmonious whole. As the Trinity is always three, yet always one, so in marriage there are to be always two, yet always one. When there are two without unity, we fail to reflect the image of God. When there is unity without diversity, when one voice is lost, we fail to reflect the image of God.

We are his workmanship, his composition. Who we are in this two-part relationship is to be an expression of who he is. Marriage is an expression of the voice of the Creator/Composer. He heard the music first within himself and then articulated it. Marriage is a manifestation, a creation of something within the Godhead. In us, God has in some measure reproduced himself. "Let us make man, male and female, in our image..." Let us make them to reflect who we are.

For further thought:

Meditate on the quote below. What do your relationships reveal about Him?

> *"No Christian has a special work to do. Our Lord calls us to no special work; he calls us to himself."*
>
> ***Oswald Chambers***[27]

---

[27] Oswald Chambers, *My Utmost for His Highest* (New York, NY: Dodd Mead & Co., 1935), October 16. Used with permission; see References.

Harmonious Voices

I find I need to frequently ask myself, "Who is the Composer, the Creator of my marriage?" There is no breaking down the wall of hostility, there is no bringing the feud to an end, there is no reconciliation, unless I first acknowledge who the Composer is and live in love and obedience to him. *He* wrote the music. *He* knows what it should sound like and how the two voices fit together in a harmonious whole. Wherever we fail as individuals to listen to the voice of the Composer, we will fail to play the music as it was intended. Whenever we fail to play in conformity to the Composer, we will produce noise, not harmony.

Suppose you were asked to play the fourth invention in the presence of Bach himself. How would you feel? How would you prepare? Would you not want to play the piece in a way that would please the composer? You would want to play the invention as Bach intended for it to be played.

Bach's hearing was said to be "so fine that he was able to detect the slightest error even in the largest ensembles...all alone, in the midst of the greatest din made by all the participants, and although he is executing the most difficult parts himself, noticing at once, whenever and wherever a mistake occurs, holding everybody together, taking precautions everywhere and repairing any unsteadiness."[28]

How like our great God, whose holiness is so fine-tuned that he can hear the slightest harshness in a relationship that he says is to be governed by love. He can hear the muttering under the breath, the mean thought we nurse, even in the din caused by a family of 10! How quickly we forget that every moment of our marriages we play in front of the Composer, who misses nothing. The Composer/Redeemer who, whenever and wherever a mistake occurs, can hold us together and repair any unsteadiness if we would but look to him. And so we begin with the truth that our Creator God is the Composer of our two-part invention and that we are playing the music, moment by moment, in his presence.

I want to go on from here and consider some of the ways we destroy the harmony, the two-part invention that God intended or composed for us. The first way is that we fail to play the music given us by the Composer. We do not like the piece assigned to us and so we choose another. We structure our marriages to meet

---

[28] Harold C. Schonberg, *The Lives of Great Composers* (New York, NY: W. W. Norton & Co., 1970), 44. Used with permission; see References.

our own needs or comfort requirements. We do not play for the Composer, we play for ourselves. We rebel against the hard places in the piece. We would rather play something simpler. Some spots in our music makes sounds we did not count on. We prefer a different sound. The sounds of loss, illness, financial problems, difficult children – these were not chords we envisioned as part of our music. We would like a piece that does not carry these within it.

What might be another way we destroy the harmony that God intended? We said earlier that marriage is diversity within unity: two voices made one. The harmony results from two independent melodies being brought together into a whole. We destroy the harmony by destroying either the unity or the diversity. In a marriage there is the coming together of two voices. There is no harmony unless both are present. One note alone does not make harmony. If one voice is missing, unity is destroyed. Is there only one voice in our marriages? When the Composer listens, who does he hear? Does the whole carry within it the notes of each of two melodies? Or are we playing a one-handed invention, which is, therefore, no invention at all?

In an invention, the two voices play different notes at different times. Sometimes one plays and then the other joins in. Sometimes the parts are played simultaneously, but rarely do both hands ever play the same note. One way to destroy the diversity of an invention is to make both hands play the same thing at the same time. Again, there is no harmony. One note is simply an octave higher or lower than the other, but each voice plays the same note. We think unity comes from being identical and division results inevitably from difference. Yet our Creator/Composer God has reconciled both through the cross, by which he put to death our hostility. He has made a way for diversity that does not divide. He has made possible a diversity that results in beautiful harmony.

It is a privilege to be given music written by the Master. We are co-laborers with him. He wrote the music and has asked us to play it as he intended it to be played. He has invited us to come alongside, to be his yoke-fellows, to labor with him to produce the creation of beauty and harmony that he envisioned. We cannot do his work unless we follow his notes (the Word) and are governed by his Spirit. The work of our Composer is sometimes a difficult work. We enter marriage saying, "For richer or poorer, in sickness and in health, for better or worse." We want and expect to be richer, healthier, and better.

You and I cannot play such difficult parts unless we know the mind of the Composer. We cannot play his music unless we follow his direction. It is only as we sit at the feet of the Master Composer that we will play the music intended for us and play it in a way that truly reflects the beauty of the music of God himself. I also firmly believe that unless you and I, as counselors, know how to sit at the feet of the Composer regarding our own marriages, we will not know how to teach others to play the pieces assigned to them. May all who watch and listen to our inventions hear a beautiful harmony that reminds them in some small way of the glorious beauty of the Composer himself.

For further thought:

What can you do to better follow the direction of our Composer?

"It needs both a meditative habit and a devout heart to believe that the trivialities of our own daily tasks speak to us of Him."

***Alexander Maclaren*[29]**

---

[29] Alexander Maclaren, *The Life of David as Reflected in His Psalms* (London: Hodder and Stoughton, 1885), 40.

Serving God in His House

What do we *want* the state of Christian counseling to be? Or perhaps, we should ask what does God himself want for us and this work that we do?

I am struck by the words in Hebrews 3:5 (NASB), "Moses indeed was faithful in all His house as a servant." The house referred to here is not Moses' house, but the House of God. You and I, as believers and those indwelt by the Holy Spirit, are the House of God. The lives we live, and certainly the work we do in the field of Christian counseling, is work done in and through the House of God. It is not our house; we did not build it; we do not own it, nor do we get to decide how it is to be governed. It is the house of another, and he decides placement, structure, function, and activities. He also gets to say what the behavior and the character of the inhabitants should look like. The phrase, "the House of God," refers to the kingship of our God and all that results from this understanding. Such thinking must be foundational to Christian counseling if it is, indeed, to be *Christian*.

We are told that Moses was *faithful* in the House of God. If we look at the history of Moses, we see that he was indeed faithful. He built the tabernacle according to the pattern God gave. The ceremonies and rituals were as God ordained. He received and interpreted the Law as God had spoken. Moses was faithful to the Word of God and to the character of God in almost all of his doings. He knew whose house it was, and he faithfully lived according to the governance *of its owner*. Moses was trusted by the Lord to live according to what He said... not what Moses thought or felt or wanted or understood. He knew whose house he was in, and he proved trustworthy to its owner.

The verse also says Moses served in God's house faithfully *as a servant*. The writer of Hebrews uses an unusual word for servant here. Interestingly enough, given our field, the Greek word is "therapon," which means one who renders voluntary service inspired by affection. The more common words refer to a bond servant or someone who runs errands, both of which could be used to describe Moses. The writer chose a word that elevates the service of Moses. Moses was a voluntary servant inspired by love. He chose to serve the Lord of the house out of love for that Lord. It carries within it the idea of cherishing the one served.

So, if we put it all together and consider what it might mean for our work, we have this: Christian counselors are those who are faithfully serving in the House of God, living under His governance in all aspects of their lives, out of sheer love for the Lord of that house. That means it is not my career, my practice, my job, my research, my book, or my class. That means faithfulness to Him when we are weary, struggling, tempted to cut corners, famous, deemed important, or ignored. It means being driven by love for God rather than outcome, reputation, fame, financial gain, or the need to feel significant.

There is one final piece to the verse that is critical. "Moses indeed was faithful in all His house as a servant, *for a testimony of those things which were afterward to be spoken.*" What is that about? It refers us back to Hebrews 1:1 where we are told God has now spoken to us in His Son. And is that not where the Word always takes us? Jesus is the builder of the house; He is the ruler of the house; he is the faithful servant of the Most High God. He is the One who has brought us truth and grace. Through him, God has spoken in a broken, bruised, and dying man who is God Himself. It is this God whom we cherish, and it is our love for him that is to motivate our work. It is this God to whom we are faithful, honoring his utter faithfulness to us and our clients. It is this God, the God of the pierced hands, whose house is our place of service. It is this God, who loved us and was faithful in all He did, who became our servant. The state of the art of Christian counseling is to be Jesus Christ. It is to be in him, through him, by him, and for him that we do this work. May he find us faithful in his entire house as adoring, loving servants.

For further thought:

Where do you believe Christian counseling to be right now? What is its drive?

> "*We are seeking to establish the Kingdom of God by the methods of men, by their policies and their programs and their machinery. The Kingdom of God can never be so established. The Kingdom of God only comes in power by way of the cross.*"
>
> ### G. Campbell Morgan[30]

---

[30] G. Campbell Morgan, *The Gospel According to Mark*, 191. Used with permission; see References.

Challenging the Culture by Having the Mind of Christ

" Having *this* mind in you, which was also in Jesus Christ..." (Philippians 2:5 NASB). These are familiar words and familiar words often lose their punch. This verse, in essence, means having a mind shaped in the same fashion as the mind of Christ – a mind governed by his priorities, thinking his thoughts, assessing every situation according to his ways, therefore sharing thoughts that are his. It means having *his* thoughts when I am under pressure, when I am at leisure, when I am in conflict, when I have been injured or accused. I daresay that if the light of God was shed into the hidden recesses of our minds, we would see many thoughts that would have no place in the mind of Christ. I suspect our minds are far fuller of our own ideas and deliberations rather than his. I also suspect we are unaware of the degree to which we are unlike Him in our thinking.

Take culture for example. You and I imbibe and inhale culture every day of our lives, from the time we are tiny until the day we die. It is truly the air we breathe. We absorb national, regional, urban, suburban, ethnic, faith, denominational, political, gender, and popular culture all the time. It goes in mindlessly. We are anesthetized to it and so we absorb the inherent toxins without awareness or consideration of the consequences. We are unseeing; it feels familiar, like home, so therefore just seems "right."

Over the last decade or so, I have been privileged to travel the world as I have done more international speaking and training. Part of that experience, of course, as most of you probably know, is that you go somewhere utterly unlike home and see things and think, "Wow, that is a different way to do family, community, worship, time, grief, food, or almost anything else you can think of." In addition, you come back home and see your life and ways through a different lens. It creates a kind of self-awareness that was lacking. If you let it, some of the anesthesia is dispelled and wakes you up to your life and things you have done thoughtlessly, without reflection, just because it was what surrounded you and done by those with whom you work, worship, or live. I have found that growing awareness to be a great, though sometimes unsettling, gift to me.

The mind of Jesus is a completely foreign culture for many of us. We are easily lulled into believing He thinks the way we do about doctrine, relationships, values, race, gender, politics, success, money, sex, power, and a host of other concerns. How subtly we slide into absorbing our own culture and somehow believing what we think is the true and sanctified version. We must follow the One who said: "My kingdom is not of this world... you are not of this world, even as I am not of this world." Jesus lived and died in a particular culture. He went to the temple, and he celebrated the Jewish holidays. I suspect he enjoyed doing so – they were, and are, rich traditions given by God. However, whenever that culture, even his religious culture, had morphed into something ungodly, he spoke out and did not follow. He discerned and named the toxins within that culture. Needless to say, such radical obedience to God over culture, comfort, and familiarity cost him a great deal. He was obviously not anesthetized. He did not swallow the surrounding cultural thoughts whole. He had eyes to see.

Do we have eyes to see? Do we recognize the toxins in the place where we live and feel safe and comfortable? Are we awake? Have we grasped how upside-down godliness looks when it is lived in this world – even in our particular Christian circles? Do we see that our ministry circles, political ideologies, denominational, or ethnic groups can, if unexamined, lead us blindly into ungodliness? Or are we convinced we are right? Do we not see or smell the toxins? It is so easy to breathe the air around us and be blind to thoughts that look nothing like Christ's because we are so used to them and they are so common – they just are, and we assume they are right. It is, after all, what our family does, what our church does or what our circles say.

Oh, I pray that the body of our Lord, whose kingdom is not of this world, will, in fact, look like its head and may our minds and cultures be rooted in His kingdom and His kingdom alone. May the legacy of our work and our lives be a growing likeness to Jesus Christ, who is himself searing light, dividing the subtle toxins from truth and the light from darkness.

For further thought:

Do we have eyes to see? Pray for wisdom, courage, and a willingness to name the ungodly things that have permeated into our cultures. May God's Church be willing to challenge the familiar and search for truth.

> *"The love of God at work in me makes me hate with the hatred of the Holy Spirit all that is not in keeping with God's holiness. To walk in the light means that everything that is of the darkness drives me closer into the center of the light."*
>
> **Oswald Chambers**[31]

---

[31] Oswald Chambers, *My Utmost for His Highest* (New York, NY: Dodd Mead & Co., 1935), December 26. Used with permission; see References.

The Least of These

Given the writings of Paul, it seems clear that the church of Jesus Christ has had divisions, angry dialogue, and exclusions since its inception. With global access to information and instant responses, there seems to be a multiplication of judgments, hatred, divisions, and demeaning words. To see such things increasing in those who say they love Christ is very sad indeed.

It is a foundational truth in the Word of our God that all human beings since the beginning of time, have been created in the image of God, knit together by the Father's hands in their mother's womb. You will *never* meet an exception to this. Whether they are male or female or of another race, healthy or sick, citizen or immigrant, rich or poor, brilliant or limited – everyone, no matter their birthplace or capacity or *unlikeness to you* is an image bearer. No matter how we choose to treat another or what language we use to describe them this fact cannot be undone.

One of the (many) current and volatile dialogues today concerns the immigrants at our borders. It is without question a critical topic. However, some of our dialogue about this topic has, frankly, been vile and grieves our God. Although we may not easily find a consensus regarding immigration, we can alter the way we dialogue – a change that might even spill over and bear fruit in other discussions.

Here are some thoughts:

1. This is a very complex problem that needs attention both now and long term. It will require bright minds with knowledge, expertise, and experience to come up with responses both short term and long term. I am certainly not one of those experts and neither, I suspect, are most of us. We can, however, call on the government to find such people and have them think, suggest, and inform those who have the power to develop wise policies and procedures both for now and for the future. The old ways are clearly not sufficient. Proverbs 11:14 (NASB) says, "Where there is no wise guidance the people fall, but in the abundance of counselors there is safety."

2. We might consider laying aside our reactivity. For example, expressing concern for immigrants is often construed as wanting open borders with no rules. It is, however, possible to be concerned about humans who are suffering and yet not think that porous borders are a wise solution. That is why wisdom and experience are necessary to think through these matters. How do we have compassion for immigrants *and* maintain the stability of our country at the same time? Choosing one without the other is neither wise nor good.

3. A second reactive response seems to be that concern for the immigrants means you are naïve and ignorant of the fact that there are some bad folks mixed in with those truly suffering. We have predators, abusers, and deceivers in our families, churches, schools, and institutions. Of course, there are some among the vulnerable and desperate ones seeking sanctuary! Such places are where predators often hide. And this fact alone should not lead to neglect of the vulnerable. In fact, it increases the urgency.

4. While we are not government and not experts, we *are* the church, the body of our Lord. It is in fact, to be our *primary* identity. The collective/prophetic voice of the church is needed today on many fronts. And our voice is, above all else, to sound like the voice of Christ – not government, politics, personal preferences, or anything else. The detention centers at our borders are full of image bearers – immigrants and border agents alike. Both groups are being traumatized. I suspect many of the immigrants were traumatized before they came. Sadly, that trauma continues here. Agents are overwhelmed and without resources. They too are traumatized and either grieving or hardening their hearts so they can endure. On all fronts damage is being done to precious people made in the image of God.

5. The immigrants lack clean water, food, clothing, and a place to lie down and sleep. Those are familiar deprivations. "I was hungry and you gave me food; I was thirsty and you gave me drink; I was naked and you clothed me...what you have done for the *least* of these, you have done for *me*" (Matthew 25:35, 40 ESV). We are

the body of our Lord here on earth. We are the present-day Word made flesh. He has been exceedingly clear about what that looks like for his people. You and I cannot literally go to the borders and do these things. We can, however, use our collective/prophetic voice to call on government to insure this happens, to ask them to allow groups like World Relief, World Vision, and many others who know how to care for the thirsty, the hungry and the naked, to go in and provide services. It will bring relief to the immigrants and to the agents.[32] The government has a huge job to do. So do we. The voice that you and I are called to heed; the voice that is to overrule all others such as the voices of tribe, race, nation, politics, or fear, is the voice of our Lord saying this: "Open your mouth for the mute, for the rights of all the unfortunate. Open your mouth, judge righteously, and defend the rights of the afflicted and needy (Proverbs 31: 8, 9 NASB).

6. Our voices need to be used respectfully and kindly to one another. Our reactivity and rancor do not sound like our Lord. We also need to raise our collective/prophetic voice in obedience to our God who came, oh so graciously, to the least of these – you and me. Perhaps such unity on our part might bestow on the immigrants – whether they stay or leave – and on the beleaguered border agents, a brief whiff of the fragrance

---

[32] Bekah McNeel, "Evangelicals Can Help at the Border. They Just Can't Do It Alone," last modified 1 July 2019, https://www.christianitytoday.com/news/2019/july/evangelicals-help-at-border-children-government-catholic-tx.html

of our God who created and loves them all. That aroma will be the sweet fragrance of Christ inviting them to seek him no matter where they live. We know for sure that that aroma will please our Lord (2 Corinthians 2:15 NIV).

For further thought:

Pray for those at the border. Pray for the government officials working there and for those working on immigration policies. Pray for the people of this nation; ask for wisdom in how to serve and love the least of these.

"He that loves the Lord Jesus Christ in sincerity must be greatly distressed that He should thus be wounded in the house of His professed friends."

John Fawcett[33]

---

[33] John Fawcett, *Christ Precious to Those Who Believe*, excerpted, Grace Gems, https://gracegems.org/28/fawcett_christ_precious3.htm (accessed 26 July 2019), Part 2, ch.3, section 7, para. 12.

Brief Meditation 7

"People who lose all their charity generally lose all their logic."

Gilbert Keith Chesterton[34]

---

[34] Gilbert Keith Chesterton, *The Everyman Chesterton* (New York, NY: Alfred A. Knopf, 1963), 872. Used with permission; see References.

Brief Meditation 8

"The result of the tragedy in Hosea's life was that he came to understand the heart of God, and what God suffered when his people sinned. He was admitted, through the mystery of his own tragedy, into an apprehension of what the sin of the nation meant against the heart of God... The pain and agony of the man's heart... have become to him an interpretation of the agony of the heart of God... He discovered what infidelity means to love."

G. Campbell Morgan[35]

---

[35] G. Campbell Morgan, *Hosea: The Heart and Holiness of God* (Eugene, OR: Wipf and Stock Publishers, 1998), 11.

Week 5

Lessons from the Every Day

I am not the first, nor will I be the last, to note how the different seasons of life afford one a fresh perspective. We were recently involved as a family in dismantling my mother's home. As many of you know, it is a difficult and complicated process, full of memories. The experience, like many in life, also carries within it some significant object lessons. One such moment for me came out of the basement of my mother's home. I have been thinking a great deal recently about such things as leadership, mentoring, and legacies. Life is short (a perspective limited to its later seasons), and it matters. What are the things that will truly matter when it is over?

One evening, weary and overwhelmed with facing the basement, I descended the stairs and was struck abruptly by a poignant image. On the far wall leaned an old metal golf cart. Next to it leaned an old wheelchair. Both were startling, as they had belonged to my father who has been gone for almost 13 years. In the first part of his life, he was a superb athlete. He swung a golf club gracefully and effortlessly. In the last 32 years of his life, he was progressively disabled, eventually unable to tie his shoes, bait his fishhook, or walk down the hallway of the nursing home. His pleasures and his suffering, both integral parts of his life, were gone, over. His love of golf and his great pain are finished.

Shortly thereafter, we were looking through boxes in the basement and I came across one that was filled with old books. Being the lover of old books that I am, I began pulling them out to see what was there. The names were familiar: Ironsides, DeHaan, Havner – saints of the faith and renowned in their time. Those books took time and hard work to write. They were published and received acclaim. They were sitting in a box in a dark basement gathering dust. I will certainly read some of them, learn from them, and be blessed. The hard work and the acclaim, both integral parts of the lives of those men, are gone. Their fame and their following are finished.

Golf carts, wheelchairs, and famous men taught me a lesson. They reminded me of truths that will never die. The things that bring us pleasure, that cause us great suffering, and that bring applause are like vapor. Poof, and they are gone. The pleasures in life are things we pursue, arrange our schedules for, and give up other things for. Suffering can be profoundly limiting; it can shut down a life, silence a voice, and slowly erode a human being. Fame – it can be intoxicating, seducing, and life distorting. We get it, we want more, and we think it speaks truth.

There is, however, in the midst of those things, a reminder of things eternal. The golf cart reminds me that joy in rightful pleasures is a gift of our Father, and merely a foretaste of the eternal pleasure and joy my earthly father now enjoys. It also reminds me that the pursuit of pleasure or excellence or discipline, all of which were part of athleticism, is never to govern a life so that love of God and others is laid aside as secondary.

The wheelchair teaches many lessons. It reminds me that suffering is awful and destructive, and we need to sit with it in all humility. It is also temporary. And it is a mystery, for a life wracked by suffering can work redemptively in this dark world, yielding demonstrations of grace, glimpses of the cross, and of the face of the One who has carried our sorrows.

And finally, fame. Fame reminds me that the world is not my judge. What does the world know of my eternal worth to the Father? And how can that world possibly assess whether or not what I have done is trustworthy? Paul says, "To me it is a very small thing that I may be examined by you, or by any human court; in fact I do not even pass verdict on myself" (1 Corinthians 4:3 NASB). The following of the crowds does not mean one is worthy, nor does their absence decree worthlessness.

Paul, in a previous verse, points us to what is eternal. "It is required of stewards that one be found trustworthy" (1 Corinthians 4:2 NASB). The pleasure, the suffering, and the fame are merely the earthly arenas in which matters are played out. If in our golf carts, our wheel-chairs, and our fame we manifest the character of the One who sits on the throne, then those mundane things become holy and we will one day hear, "Well done, good and faithful servant."

For further thought:

How have the pleasures of this life reminded you of the beauty of the Father? How have you been able to see glimpses of the cross in the sorrows of life?

> *"His people are to be powerfully drawn after Him and attached to Him in all the conditions of life into which they may be brought."*
>
> ***John Fawcett***[36]

---

[36] John Fawcett, *Christ Precious to Those Who Believe*, excerpted, Grace Gems, https://gracegems.org/28/fawcett_christ_precious3.htm (accessed 26 July 2019), Part 2, ch.3, section 10, para. 27.

Three-Legged Race

Did you ever participate in a three-legged race? They usually occur in elementary school or at a kid's party. The left leg of one partner is tied to the right of the other and they put their arms around each other's waists. The object is for the partners to run without falling over. It seems easy, but it takes practice to make two legs from different bodies work as one... sounds a little bit like marriage to me.

I find it interesting that when we write about or discuss marriage, we most often do so by talking about the two separate parts (husband and wife) and focus on what each ought to be doing. Husbands should be this way; wives should be that way. And there is often a veiled threat lurking in the background that if you are not the kind of spouse being described, your marriage may be somehow compromised. We do not seem to speak often about the "us."

Think about the three-legged race. If you do not support one another with your arms, you will not be able to work together as one because your bodies will be pulling different directions and hinder your race. You *each* need to put out one arm toward the other. It needs to stay there holding on for the *entire* race. One alone will not work nearly so well.

You also need to be facing the same direction. Can you imagine trying such a race with one facing backwards and the other forward? You would not have a shared goal in sight. One would be going one way and the other a different way... or both would be going the same way but the one facing backwards would not be operating effectively.

Your legs are tied together. Each contributes a different leg – one is left, the other right. So, differences are joined together for a single purpose. The legs are different, the feet are most likely different sizes and agility, strength and speed may not be equal. There are a lot of potential differences being tied together! The coordination required by both means studying each other and mutually making adaptations so the two become one for the purpose of running well and reaching the goal without falling down. It will demand practice and involve frustration, energy, focus, and lots of laughter. The "we" is the central point.

I suspect attitude matters, too. How would you like to compete in a three-legged race with a partner who does nothing but tell you what you are doing wrong? You know how those statements that go, "If you... then we." Or how about running the race with someone who keeps dropping his or her arm, so the unity was utterly dependent on you alone? One partner cannot do all the holding. Or what about a partner whose eyes keep straying from the goal, wandering off, not seeing you and tending toward another instead of the one to whom he or she is joined?

Clearly the focus has to be on the fact that there are two individuals with different capacities and skills and each of them must work with the other, so those capacities strengthen the union itself. Anything solely self-centered will hinder the race. One cannot do anything that will not affect the other. The goal is to finish the race as one, without falling down.

You see, if we think about it, we might suggest that we are in a three-legged race with Jesus. We are members of His body, of His flesh, and of His bones (Ephesians 5:30 NIV). We are tied together, joined, and running for the one goal that matters. We are to run with endurance the race set before us, with Jesus, the author and finisher of our faith (Hebrews 12:1 NASB). Christ began the race; He finished the race; and now with Him, we press toward the goal. We are united to Him as one – running together, joined and flesh of His flesh. His arm is around us and He longs for ours to be around Him. He has not told *me* to run the race; He says *we* will run the race. Run with Me, he says. I will never leave you or forsake you. When you fall, I will lift you up. Face the same direction I do. Pursue the same goal with Me and when we cross the finish line, you will enter into glory with a crown on your head.

Oh, that our marriages would be enough like the three-legged race that they might, in some measure, reflect to the world the race we are running with our

Lord. "Two are better than one, because they have good reward for their labor and if either of them falls, the one will lift up his or her companion" (Ecclesiastes 4:9-10 NASB).

For further thought:

Meditate on the quote below. Is there anything that could be causing you to stumble as you walk with Him?

"Endeavor resolutely to be of the number of those who have the highest affinity with the Son of Man...walking with Him the rough road."

G. Campbell Morgan[37]

---

[37] G. Campbell Morgan, *The Gospel According to Mark*, 86. Used with permission; see References.

Divisions, Deceptions, and Disease

A theologian prayed that his life would make the presence of the person of God clearer for others. He feared living a life that somehow obscured the presence of Jesus for others. I fear that we as the body of Christ today are doing much to obscure the splendor of the presence of God in our midst. I have been reading Paul's letters to the Corinthians and been struck by their relevance to the present-day church.

Corinth was a great city in the Roman Empire. It was wealthy and lustful. It was known for the clever arguments of its resident philosophers. The delivery of such arguments was of the highest form, and it was the center of all things intellectual. The city was also rotten at its core, corrupt, and lewd. The body of Christians in that city were meant to be characterized by righteousness, sanctity, and the fruits of redemption. Instead,

133

they had taken God's name while departing from him and his ways, gathering around their own views and ideas. They were centered on the philosophies of the hour and created within the church schisms based on opinions. They were focused on the material, having lost their understanding of the spiritual. There was moral failure in the church, as wrong thinking easily leads to wrong-doing. The sin in their midst was ignored, covered up, and they failed to deal with it by bringing it to the light and grieving over it. Sound uncomfortably familiar?

We have caused divisions and arguments by adamantly using labels to define the place of women in the home and the church. We identify ourselves by those words; "I am this or I am that." We have divisions over issues of justice. Justice is what the church is called to, or justice is not the church's call – evangelism is the only call. We have been and continue to be divided over race. We say, "they," which means "not us." We treat "them" with disdain, disrespect, and distance. We tolerate bullying, rage, arrogance, and sexual sin in our leaders. We have ignored and covered up sin, saying we are protecting "the work of God." And now that such evil is being exposed, we somehow think a rule will prevent it – as in never letting men and women work or dialogue together. If rules could prevent humans from sin, God would have delivered the Ten Commandments to Moses and sat down. And frankly, if we follow that rule, we will build more chasms between male and female in the body of Christ. Not to mention there are those in power who also abuse boys and young men. We have divisions over politics – in the church of Jesus Christ! It has infected the church with a warfare of words. We are focused on the material and are losing our understanding of the spiritual. Our Lord said, "*My* kingdom is *not* of this world." It is not in human governments or human groups or human ideas. Jesus' kingdom is formed by leaving *all* and following – not ideas – but *Him*.

Paul calls the church in Corinth to God's wisdom which is always displayed in righteousness, sanctification, and the fruit of redemption. By righteousness he means conformity to Christ. That means we look like him; we bear his fragrance. I fear we do not bear his image and we have indeed obscured his splendor before the watching world. By sanctification Paul means progress in the character of Christ. That means I should be growing in love, kindness, self-control, truth, and justice, for these are characteristics of my Lord. I am to be increasingly demonstrating the fruit of redemption until the day comes when we fully escape from the bondage of sin.

We have been deceived. We have believed that size and fame and numbers are proof of the presence of God. In doing so we have protected institutions instead of sheep and fostered arrogance rather than humility. Paul showed deep concern over the church that was covering up sin and the influence of that cover-up on God's people. We have believed that controlling human government is more important than obedience to the government of God over our lives. We scream hateful words, both literally and via social media, at those who do not agree with our stance as if the "right" human government determines what our God can do. We think that rigid adherence to stringent rules separating men and women in the name of propriety will control human hearts. Yet our God clearly says our wrongdoing comes *from our hearts,* not from those around us. We have thought our race, our community, our nation, our way of thinking is superior, rather than seeking desperately to develop the mind of Christ about all things. *Anything* that deflects the mind from the centrality of Jesus Christ and his cross is of the flesh. He, and he alone, is made unto us wisdom. Then and only then will the diseases infecting the people of God be cured.

You want to be a safe and holy shepherd who feeds his sheep? Then feed on him only – not the position, the applause, the growth, or fame. Feed on him so you can teach *his* sheep to do the same as they go out to minister in his name (character). You want women, men, girls, and boys to be safe with those who have power? An immoral woman of the "wrong" race was utterly safe with Jesus – who broke all the rules in sitting alone with her. She was safe because he sought to do *only* the will of his father. No one in his world was a "them" unless they chose to be so. And it is very sobering to see that those who did that all the way to the cross were religious leaders. They treated *him* as a "them." They excommunicated the Lord of glory. The man Christ Jesus served neither Rome nor Israel. He bowed to no government or human institution – secular or religious. He called both to truth and light.

The call to the church of Jesus Christ today is to fall on our faces, seeking him and asking him to search our hearts and lives. You and I are all ministers to the world in Jesus' name. The word for minister in the New Testament means under-rower. Yes, a galley slave on a warship who does not obey wind or weather or waves but rows ever and always according to the instructions of the captain. When each under-rower lives fully under the authority of that captain then that ship can survive battles, storms, and weariness as they row together under the command of one.

Oswald Chambers has taught me many things. He says, "We count as service what we do in the way of Christian work; Jesus Christ calls service *what we are to Him*. Discipleship is based on devotion to Jesus Christ."[38] We have substituted ideas and opinions, institutions and groups, for allegiance to the Person of Jesus Christ and his Word. His *first* obedience was always to the will of the Father, no matter the cost. May we, the body of Christ today, be known for our devotion, our love and obedience to Christ – under-rowers whose service is never dictated by current ideas, or groups, or causes – but within those spheres we are first and foremost devoted to the Crucified Christ. It is then and only then that we will make His presence known to others.

---

[38] Oswald Chambers, *My Utmost for His Highest* (New York, NY: Dodd Mead & Co., 1935), June 19. Used with permission; see References.

For further thought:

Where have you seen divisions and deceptions cloud the presence of God? What are steps that can be taken to re-devote ourselves and our work to the Lord?

> *"The Corinthian church lost its vision of the Divine purpose in building because men gathered around individuals. They lost their vision of the whole and were obsessed by the partial...No other foundation can ever be laid than Jesus Christ."*
>
> **G. Campbell Morgan**[39]

---

[39] G. Campbell Morgan, *The Corinthian Letters of Paul: An Exposition on I and II Corinthians* (Grand Rapids, MI: Fleming H. Revell, Co., 1946), 59. Used with permission; see References.

The Forces that Shape Us

The clients who come to us live in this world. They also live in a society that ignores and denigrates God. Many know him not at all or only very little. They are in pain, and they want something to ease it – yesterday. People believe that suffering makes them useless, and so their pain must be eliminated at any cost. If onc is suffering one cannot produce, and if one cannot produce, one is worthless. Those who suffer feel isolated and disconnected. Some have grown up without ever seeing or experiencing a loving relationship between two people who respect each other. They long for such a relationship yet have no idea how to build one. They have been spoon-fed on seven-minute sound bites and have little understanding of waiting, stillness and endurance. They have heard that therapy makes people feel better or heals wounds, and so they come.

You and I cannot respond to those in our culture in healing and holy ways unless we have learned how to resist the great forces which surround us. We are creatures, and it is the nature of creatures to be shaped, to change. Only God is unchangeable. We *will* be shaped by our culture or made in its image, unless we learn those things which will enable us to be in the culture, but not of it.

Knowing God

The first thing we must learn is to know God. By that I do not simply mean acquiring knowledge about God. Such an exercise can be carried out by those shaped by the culture. Almost anyone can collect facts. Scripture indicates that we can know God in quite a different way. To know him means to seek after him, to understand his thoughts, to love him, to obey him, to be shaped by him until we look like him. That is radically different from acquiring a boat-load of information *about* him.

To know God includes loving him with all our heart, soul, and mind. To love God in this way means that all our person and all areas of our lives will be permeated by his character and his presence. As we pursue him, our lives will be governed by his Word and his Spirit. When we belong to him, we will begin to look like him.

To love God with all our mind means that we will begin to have the mind of Christ. We can then study with a discerning mind the discipline of psychology, the theories of counseling, the critiques of such theories, and the culture in which they are embedded. God created the world so it could be studied. The work of the Spirit in us enables us to study that world and the creatures who inhabit it so that we learn to think God's thoughts after him.

Waiting Before God

In order to be light in this dark world, you and I must also learn to wait. If we know how to wait that means we know how to stay in place; to watch expectantly; to remain stable. We live in a world full of violence, impulsivity, and instability. We work with people who have experienced the destructive consequences of such things in their lives. We cannot create an atmosphere that breathes the life of God unless we know how to wait, unless we know the discipline of staying power. Waiting repairs the damage done to us by the fret and noise of our world. If we cannot wait, how can we listen? If we cannot wait, how will we hear and understand? If we do now know how to wait, what will keep us from impulsively reacting in a moment of crisis? If we cannot wait, what will stay our tongues when we are inclined to rashness?

To learn to wait quietly before God and his word is to hear him speak. We cannot obey unless we hear his Word. To sit in his presence day after day is to learn of him. How can we become like him if we do not know who he is? To wait on him is to be given strength when we are weary and power when we are weak. So often when we are weak and powerless, rather than wait, we push ourselves to act. Crises make us weary. Death and suffering around us often render us powerless. The discipline of placing ourselves in the presence of God and waiting on him, will infuse us with the life of God and strengthen us to enter into alarm moments anointed by his Spirit.

Standing in Relationships

We also must learn to stand against the forces of our culture that would shape us into disconnected people. We were created to be in relationship. To live isolated, disconnected lives is to live in opposition to our Creator's intention. Counseling behind closed doors, late-night writing and research projects and the perennial rush of things all conspire to keep us working, accomplishing and isolated. Our God has called us to communion, fellowship, and love for one another. Like waiting on God, such things take time.

How can we do therapeutic relationships wisely and well, if we do not nurture our own with vigilance? We will either offer less of ourselves than we should or begin to prey upon those who come to us to meet our needs. Do we really think we can teach others about relationships of any kind if we are not continually "going to school" with others and before God regarding our own? We need relationships to help us see ourselves accurately. "Iron sharpens iron; so a man sharpens the countenance of his friend (to show rage or worthy purpose)" (Proverbs 27:17 AMP). It is within the context of relationships that who we are is revealed. Relationships keep us from fooling ourselves about who we are. The technology and busyness of our age mean that maintaining relationships of significance is a matter of swimming upstream. To fail to do so is to be less than God intended.

Learning the Art of Stillness

If the foundation of our lives is anything but worship of the Lamb, then our lives will be askew. The emphasis of our age is on the work, rather than on the person of the worker. Worship places us in our rightful position. We are creatures bowing in homage to the Creator. To worship him as Creator and to remember our place as his creatures frees us to work according to the principles of his kingdom, rather than according to the goals or viewpoints of our culture, either secular or Christian.

The place of worship reminds us that Jesus Christ alone is the Redeemer, and we are his servants. The place of worship strips us of our arrogance and reminds us that our systems, our profession, and our position are worthless unless they emanate from love for God. It is only then that our great fear of inadequacy falls away, and we stand before God possessing nothing but a worshipful awareness of him. This will often result in our being fools in the eyes of our culture, but as creatures of the Almighty God, we will not be determined by our culture. God's aim is that we be holy at all costs, and then as his holy children go out into our world and our profession permeated by the aroma of his presence.

For further thought:

Set aside all books and technology and be still. Listen for the Voice of God. Then pray for patience as you wait to see what He is doing in your life.

> *"Beware of any work for God which enables you to evade concentration on him. A great many Christian workers worship their work. The snare of Christian workers is making eyes at spiritual success. Never court anything other than the approval of God."*
>
> **Oswald Chambers**[40]

---

[40] Oswald Chambers, *My Utmost for His Highest* (New York, NY: Dodd Mead & Co., 1935), April 23. Used with permission; see References.

Breaking Faith or Bearing Fruit?

Divorce. It is an ugly word... a sad word. It is about something breaking or fracturing and can involve neglect, bruising, or a break in the wall of unity. It is a violation of someone or something that was once whole. We in the Christian world have primarily used the word for the end of a marriage in the courts of law and have taken the words of Malachi and said, "God hates divorce." Which, indeed, He does. However, I would suggest that we have not understood our God clearly in this area. We have severely limited His words to us and in doing so have limited our obedience to Him.

Most certainly, since the beginning, our God created man and woman in relationship. God said, "Let us make man in our image, *after our likeness*: and let *them* have dominion over... the earth" (Genesis 1:26 ESV). He created a "them" – single, yet plural – which means relationship. They were different and yet they were one. He told *them together* to bear fruit – which certainly means across all spectrums of human life, not just children. Multiply – make more of the beauty, the good that I have made... make more in My likeness. Fill the earth with My likeness. Take care of it and command it for good. They were blessed abundantly by God so they, in turn, might bless each other, the earth and succeeding generations... multiplying the likeness of God everywhere they went.

God directed humans to rule the earth and the creatures on it but said nothing about ruling each other. Ruling was for things outside the relationship, done jointly, and the outcome was to bear fruit and a subdued and nurtured world. Power was used to bless both each other and the world... and it was good. In Genesis 2, we get some more information. Aloneness was declared not good, and a corresponding helper was needed. In essence, we have two servants joined together to produce and bear fruit, both living under the government of God. Instead, humans ignored the governance of God in their lives and put themselves in the place of power. They took it upon themselves to rule their choices, decisions, and each other. As a result, multiplying and bearing fruit of any kind became painful for all. By putting themselves in the place of God – seeking what they wanted rather than what He wanted – the joining of two as one is now marred. Divorce, wearing many different faces, entered the world.

Let's do a bit of a word study. The word divorce means disunion (the breaking of something) or a breach (a violation). It means to sever or separate something or to neglect or cause a gap in the wall. "Little" divorces happen all the time in many marriages – for years. How many times can skin be ruptured and still heal? How many times can a wall of protection be destroyed before it cannot be built again? We have lost sight of the fact that our God hates divorces of all sizes and kinds.

Is it divorce to hide away every evening while looking at pornography behind a shut door and ignoring both wife and family? Is it divorce to batter a spouse with objects, fists, or words? Is it divorce to bar your spouse from any access to money? Is it divorce to pour out rage and humiliation on your family and deceitfully present a different face at church? Have you not, in the words of Malachi, broken faith with your spouse and acted both treacherously and deceitfully?

God says, "For I hate sending away... and he who hath covered violence with his clothing..." (Malachi 2:16 AMP). Do not all of the previously mentioned involve a sending away? Where did we get the idea that the only thing we can call divorce is a piece of paper provided by a secular court?

Years ago, I had a phone conversation with a pastor about a woman in his church who was being beaten and finally fled on foot in her robe at night to the police station. We found a safe house for her, and I advised her not to return home to her husband. She did not. The pastor who called me told me I was wrong not to urge her to return to her husband. I responded, "She has no husband." You see, to husband another is to preserve, save or safeguard. Jesus says His Father is the husbandman of the vineyard (John 15 NIV). He nurtures that vineyard, so it is protected and bears abundant fruit. Any behavior in a relationship that does not look like Him is a rupture to that bond, whether it is words, fists, coercion, or an abuse of power. Our God does, indeed, hate divorce, violence, deceit, rage, or violations of any kind.

We have undoubtedly misled many suffering people with our rigid interpretation of what God hates. In doing so, we have contributed to the damage of precious people created in the image of God and confused them about who He is and what He says. Also, we have failed those who abuse because we have minimized and glossed over matters that God hates, thereby not always preparing them a pathway for repentance, redemption, and reconciliation. We have not always protected the vulnerable, nor have we always confronted the abusive. Many times, we leave marriages saturated with sin and deceit without truth or care because we value the external appearance of marriage over the holiness of God lived out in hidden places.

In marriage, we are meant by God to oversee His world and multiply His likeness and beauty in all that we do – bearing fruit that carries the fragrance of Christ even behind closed doors. The Bible commands us not to break faith with God (Numbers 5:6, Joshua 22:16 ESV), and He promises to never break faith with us (Psalm 89:33 NASB). As people helpers, let us courageously and compassionately live out the gracious and loving ministry of reconciliation He has given us (2 Corinthians 5:18 NIV) and encourage marriage partners not to break faith with their sacred covenant.

For further thought:

What are your thoughts on this reflection on marriage, divorce, and husbandry?

"What is the process of mislaying God? Giving an intellectual assent to the fact of his existence, i.e. doctrine, without seeing to it that our conduct corresponds with our assent. Intellectual orthodoxy will blast a man as surely as heresy will unless there is the action in life that corresponds with the assent of the mind to truth."

G. Campbell Morgan[41]

---

[41] G. Campbell Morgan, *Hosea: The Heart and Holiness of God,* 90.

Brief Meditation 9

"Not only must our relationship to God be right but our external expression of that relationship must be right."

***Oswald Chambers*[42]**

---

[42] Oswald Chambers, *My Utmost for His Highest* (New York, NY: Dodd Mead & Co., 1935), July 31. Used with permission; see References.

Brief Meditation 10

"God's servant has been sent forth, weak and gentle, with quiet methods and to very slow effects. What chance has such, our service, in the ways of the world, where to be forceful and selfish, to bluster and battle, is to survive and overcome. So we speak, and the panic ambition rises to fight the world with its own weapons and to employ the kinds of debate, advertisement and competition by which the world goes forward."

George Adam Smith[43]

---

[43] George Adam Smith, *The Expositor's Bible: The Book of Isaiah Volumes I and II* (London: Hodder and Stoughton Publishers, 1890), 269.

Week 6

Going By Way of the Cross

If we look at the life of Jesus, we see that the incarnation led to redemption by way of the cross. If the perfect Son of God had to go that way, it is unlikely you and I will be excused. To go by way of the cross, of course, speaks of many things. One of the things the cross does is give us the truth about what God thinks. The cross teaches us that this world, and those of us who inhabit it, are so hideously dark and wrong that only the death of God himself could remedy it. The cross also demonstrates a depth of love for the unlovable utterly beyond our comprehension. It is a startling exhibition of the heart of God. In the cross we have an eternal symbol of God's point of view.

I have come to see that the only way I can hope to look like Jesus and bring life to others is by way of the cross. If I do not go by way of the cross and have put to death the things in me that are not of God, then those things will put to death the things that are of God, in me and in those whose lives I touch. There are five specific ways, disciplines, that God continues to use to create his life in me.

Worship

The discipline of worship reminds me that God is God. The discipline of worship is what keeps me from being shaped by the evil and suffering I confront on a daily basis. We are profoundly shaped by what we worship. None is worthy of our worship but the Lamb that was slain. The discipline of worship reminds me that God is holy and just, though this world is teeming with evil and injustice. Worship reminds me that he who is high and lifted up also dwells with the humble and broken, and that because of the cross, none of us, no matter how small or crushed, need be afraid. Worship takes me into the very presence of God. The power of the healing force of the presence of God then shapes me so that I am changed to look like, to bear the image of, the one I worship.

Truth

The discipline of truth as seen at the cross is that I am guilty of abuse. I, who react with shock, surprise, and disdain for perpetrators also abuse or violate others. I, who find abuse of children with one's genitals incomprehensible, have abused others with my tongue. The ground at the foot of the cross is indeed level. The discipline of truth helps me see who I am before God, lest I become haughty and blinded to my own mistreatment of others. The discipline of truth prevents me from getting filled up with hate or condescension toward perpetrators, lest an arrogant rage cause me to mislead others in the way they confront the evil that is in their lives. The discipline of truth keeps me ever before God, pleading with the psalmist, "Keep your servant from presumptuous or arrogant sins; cleanse me from secret, hidden sins" (Psalm 19:13 NASB). The discipline of truth ever reminds me that no matter how much I know or how many people I help, that I am ever a learner, a disciple undergoing training. I am not the Teacher. I am only a servant of the Teacher.

Study

The discipline of study keeps me ever a student, one who listens, examines, and pays attention. The study of God's Word in its proper sense, keeps me from simply acquiring more and more knowledge, and causes me to continually bow before what I learn, so that my Teacher might work in me what his life and death have taught me. The ongoing study of human beings keeps me listening acutely, so that my responses, verbal and non-verbal, might be wise, loving, and timely applications of the truth of God.

Prayer

Prayer does not seem to be anything we do naturally or easily. It is, however, a discipline Jesus modeled for us and exhorted us to do. Jesus was continually in contact with God through prayer and we are called to do the same. As the years pass, I find I am coming to view prayer in quite a different way than previously. I used to think of prayer as a way of getting things from God.

However, if I consider prayer by looking at the cross, I find that my former view is backwards. Prayer is not about God indulging my spiritual propensities, as if somehow I needed things to go my way in order to serve him. Rather, prayer is for the purpose of getting to know God and developing God's life in me.

Obedience

We cannot be conductors of the life of God to others unless that life permeates, shapes, our very being. Death is transformed into life only by the work of the Spirit of God in a life. If the result of truth, worship, study, and prayer is not obedience, then death will reign. Our lives will not be redemptive in the lives of others unless we have learned to bow to God's work of redemption in us. Obedience results in lives that explain the grace and truth of the Father to others. Obedience results in lives that are used to buy back others from the realm of death in the name of Jesus. Obedience results in lives that bear the image of Jesus.

You and I were created by the Almighty God to be image-bearers. Those things which surround us imprint us with their image. We, in turn, impact others. The principle is this: we become like that which we habitually reflect. Unless we all with unveiled face reflect the character of our Lord, so that we are hourly being transformed into God's likeness, we will be likely to catch the soul disease with which we are working instead of helping to cure it. As sinners who serve as therapists to those both devastated by the evil of others and yes, are also evil themselves, we will not survive unless we know how to become like the cedars of Lebanon. Their most striking characteristic is that instead of feeding parasites, the strength of the life within these trees is so great, it kills the parasites. May we learn from God how to be so filled with God's life and how to so clearly bear God's image that like the cedars of Lebanon, our very existence destroys those things that are of the nature of death. May our work in the dark and painful places of others' lives be a redemptive work because, bearing God's image in our person, God's life is being poured out through us all the time.

For further thought:

Which of these five disciplines do you feel most comfortable with? Which of these five disciplines do you struggle with the most?

"Because you have such a work to do in such a field, do not become mindless. Do not become such by a permitted habit of forgetfulness, deepening until it fixes."

Bishop Moule[44]

---

[44] Bishop Moule, *Ephesian Studies: Expository Readings on the Epistle of Saint Paul to the Ephesians* (New York, NY: Hodder and Stoughton, 1900), 270-271.

Yielding to the Lordship of Christ

Expertise is the quality that challenges those in leadership positions to define themselves in terms of their abilities. A good leader is someone who is an "expert," perpetually acquiring more information and demonstrating that acquisition by an ever-increasing proficiency.[45] Counselors are expected to have a wide range of knowledge, remain well-read on all the research, be able to write and sell books, speak effectively at presentations and seminars, and simultaneously be filled with wisdom, compassion, insight, and something almost magical that helps people change quickly. Within this context, leadership is then reduced to a

---

[45] Edwin Friedman, *Generation to Generation: Family Process in Church and Synagogue* (New York, NY: The Guilford Press, 2011).

never-ending treadmill of obtaining more knowledge and a better skill set. The second quality of a good leader is charisma. Charismatic leaders can unify divided bodies, motivate depressed people to change, infect others with enthusiasm, and galvanize people into action.[46]

When the demands are great and the pressure is on, a leader can be seduced into obedience to the work at hand and equate that to their obedience to Christ. Decisions can be made based on what will succeed, bring notoriety, or produce greater numbers or change. And, of course, such things are not necessarily bad or wrong in and of themselves – more people in the caseload, more knowledge for a terrific book, or a glowing reputation. How can such things be bad? Corruption only begins when they become the master. We are not called to love and obedience to the "work" and its demands, but to Jesus Christ... and Him alone. When we allow leadership demands to determine character rather than Christlikeness then we have traded masters. This wayward master of leadership is not concerned with character, but with outcomes. The master of work is not focused on whether we are a delight to the heart of the Father, but whether or not our leadership is declared a success by others.

If we are honest, all of us have wrestled with this issue at one time or another. There is a great pull to live hierarchically – with the work we are gifted and called

---

[46] Edwin Friedman, *Generation to Generation: Family Process in Church and Synagogue.*

to do being primary and all the rest of life arranged around and below it. We rationalize that it is, after all, God's work. We are doing it for Him. He has gifted and called us to the work. It has eternal value. There is, however, a major flaw in this line of thinking, for according to the Scriptures, the foundational premise is not ministry *for* God *but God Himself.* All of life is not to be arranged around and below leadership. All of life is to be arranged around and below love and obedience to a preeminent God, including whatever work or role He has called us to. The Scriptures say we are to love God with everything we have *and then* do the work.

All leaders are followers. Many follow the call of the culture, secular and Christian, in which they live. Our Lord also followed, even as He led. He said, "I do exactly as the Father commanded Me" (John 14:31 NASB). He was not governed by the calls to kingship or the needs of the people. He followed the voice of His Father alone and, in doing so, showed us how to lead without blindly bearing the pattern of the era in which we live. Contrary to the belief that bigger and more is a better result and the primary proof of success, Jesus came and used the common to point to the precious. The value of what humans do is not predicated on the arena or audience or by measured success but determined by the presence or the fragrance of the precious. Consider the value of being common men and women (as our God became a man in the flesh) – doing common things in your common lives – but do so seeking Christ, full of His life so that all those common, ordinary things will be permeated with the life of the Living One. This is leadership patterned after Christ.

What does Jesus do? He allows the little hour, the little mission, to eclipse the great one. He, who has already humbly bowed to humanity in a transforming way by becoming common flesh himself, bows yet lower and meets the simple need of the moment. It is a small thing, even by human standards, for it is merely a deficiency in the physical provisions for the feast. And the Scriptures say, "The beginning of His signs Jesus did in Cana of Galilee, and *manifested His glory*, and His disciples *believed* in Him" (John 2:11 NASB). The little mission was allowed to eclipse the great one and, in doing so, the great one was still accomplished. The "little" mission of our marriages, our parenting, our relationships, our thought lives, our tone of voice, or our small acts of kindness are the very places where Jesus can manifest His glory – indeed, where He desires to manifest His glory and thereby lead others to believe in Him.

Nothing... *nothing* should govern us except love and obedience to Jesus Christ. When the goal of leadership guides us to disregard family, ignore the least of these, speak harshly, find the common things an annoyance, and the little missions as beneath us, then we have failed to follow the God we claim to serve. All of us are susceptible to using what God has given and then becoming disobedient to Him. Whenever we allow the demands of ministry to override obedience to God, then we have failed to follow our Savior. The gifts of God only bring glory to Him when they are used from a place of obedience.

Some years ago, I was wrestling with God about the idea of leadership and influence, asking how to do such things in a way that was truly pleasing to him. God led me to John 17:19 (NASB), "For *their* sakes I sanctify myself, that they themselves also may be sanctified in truth." In other words, He helped me understand for the sake of the sheep I am made holy, so that they also may be made holy. Do you want to lead the people of God in a way that bears fruit for eternity? Do you want to see the glory of God made manifest in the little missions of your life? Then bow down to yield to Christ in the crevices and corners of your life until he has made you to look like himself – holy and obedient to the Father no matter where you are. Godly leadership is ultimately about our relationship to the Master.

For further thought:

What are your gifts? Are they used to serve the masters of leadership, work, etc., or for Christ? How can we use our gifts to please him?

> *"The principle of godly rule is the most important one. It is this: the seeking to help, not to lord; to keep from wrong paths and lead into right paths; for the glory of God and the good of those guided, not for the gratification of the ruler. Such rule always leads the ruler to the Cross and saves the ruled at the cost of the ruler."*
>
> **Hudson Taylor[47]**

---

[47] Howard Taylor, *The Spiritual Secret of Hudson Taylor* (New Kensington, PA: Whitaker House, 1996).

When the Prince of Peace Calls

I have often found that traveling and teaching cross-culturally has opened my eyes and led to reflecting on things I have settled in an unexamined way. Many of my experiences have seemed like parables written by the hand of God to teach me more about His ways and thoughts. A recent trip to the Middle East was no exception.

Our younger son worked in Abu Dhabi for two years or so for a member of the royal household. They met in Washington and our son had served as a consultant to this man. A friendship developed and an invitation to continue working together was the result. After he had been there a while, we were invited to visit the country as guests of His Highness to see our son and be introduced to the country and culture. Plans were made, but at the last minute we were asked to leave a few days earlier than expected as the prince's schedule changed, and he wanted to be in the country to meet us when we arrived. When the call came through – knowing it would upset schedules and impact many people – our immediate response was to say, "Of course." The prince had called; we would come. No thought required. It would impact others, but the response was still certain and sure.

Therein lies the first lesson. How often has my Lord, the King of heaven and earth, called to me and I have equivocated, delayed or, even at times, refused? The question had to be asked, "Would I do for an earthly prince what I would not do for my King?"

We went – fancy airline, plush seats, great food – and were met at the airport by our son and whisked away to the palace to meet the prince. As a female walking into a room full of Arab men, I went over protocol very carefully with our son – wait to be greeted, do not speak first, the prince will stay seated, do not offer my hand, and do not sit until directed. To my son's knowledge, no other female had ever been in that room... and he spent almost every evening there, so he knew.

We arrived and were escorted in. The room was occupied by about 15 Arab men in full regalia. My husband and I walked in and, no sooner had we done so, the prince stood, walked over to us quickly and extended his hand to me warmly. He greeted me by name, introduced himself by his first name, and showed me to the seat at his right hand. All 15 men followed his example. They did what their prince did. Needless to say, we were greatly honored and graciously welcomed.

What a small taste, but a true one, of the Lord of heaven and earth seated on the throne – who will, and does even now, welcome us into the throne room with grace and glory. The Arab prince did it because he loves my son and is a gracious man. Rather than using his power to keep me in my place (something he had every right to do), he broke through his titles and fortifications and entered my space. He crossed over a stunning number of boundaries: religion, gender, economics, position, and ethnicity.

The Lord of all heaven and earth does the same at great cost to himself – his own life – and so by his blood I enter and stand received with all grace. Common enough doctrine. Grace has become too common, perhaps, and we are so familiar with it that we are no longer awed. I was stunned by the earthly prince who crossed over position, tradition, gender, culture, religion, and training to greet me with his hand. That experience has taught me, reminded me, of the awe due to my true Lord who, at a cost beyond measure, welcomes me, crossing over the barriers of highest position and glory, as well as those of sin and death, to welcome me at the right hand of the Father.

This experience has also reminded me of the grace with which we are to do our work – humbly crossing over human barriers, prejudices, fears, and judgments – to enter into the lives of those we counsel, graciously welcoming them into our space and time and with respect and kindness entering into theirs. How easy it is to be governed by our culture, bias, feelings, a particular diagnosis, or preferences. Such barriers between humans are to fall down and we are called, as servants of the Most High King, to enter into foreign territory, even hostile places, full of grace and truth.

For further thought:

Would you do for an earthly prince what you would not do for our King?

"Behold the Priest, love stooping to the very uttermost depth to deal with the poison and the virus to undermine the awful structure of evil that has been erected."

G. Campbell Morgan[48]

---

[48] G. Campbell Morgan, *Studies in the Prophecy of Jeremiah*, 211. Used with permission; see References.

Measuring Greatness in the Kingdom of God

What is the condition for greatness in the kingdom of God? That seems like a pretty important question, doesn't it? In essence, what does it take to be great in the greatest kingdom of time and eternity?

If we look around the faith community today, there seem to be some who have achieved greatness. They are respected, followed, lauded, and raised high. They are articulate, charismatic, read by thousands, and verbally powerful. They are known. However, such lives do not provide us with the answer. In response to the question raised by his disciples, who while jostling for greatness, nevertheless asked a highly significant question, Jesus placed a little child in their midst. Apparently, Jesus measures greatness differently in his kingdom.

In our kingdoms greatness is measured by high position, fame, money, and power. No child would qualify.

As a matter of fact, children would get trampled in such a kingdom. And indeed they do. In our efforts to achieve what we call greatness, we ignore, use, humiliate, and fail our children in many ways, including complicity in covering such things as abuse when exposure threatens our coveted greatness.

You see, Jesus measures greatness on the level of soul not size. We can have large-sized trappings and be known as great. Jesus wants a great soul known to be like him and he became little. He put the child in the middle and said unless you get down here you cannot achieve greatness.

So how do we know if we are like a child? How do we know if we have achieved greatness in the kingdom of God? He told us the answer quite clearly: if we are like the child, we will receive the child. In addition, he says that those who hurt children or cause them to stumble are exposed as not having a child heart.

When we turn our eyes away, close our hearts, deny truth for the sake of comfort or fame; when we under any circumstances respond in a way that does not receive, nurture, or protect a child, we actually destroy not only the child but also ourselves. Jesus says in making such choices it would have been *to our profit* to have a millstone around our necks and be drowned in the sea. The offender will make more in the economy of God by such a death than he ever will if he offends a child.

The child-heart receives the child. Those without a child-heart offend the child or protect those who do. Those who receive the child also receive Jesus. Those who do not receive the child offend Jesus. Our treatment of children, in public or in secret, is an exposure of the size of our souls. Given the statistics about child abuse in the faith community and the staggering failure of leaders, parents, and religious institutions to protect the children, I would say that we have very few great souls among us today. We can test our own souls by our relationship to children.

The great souls among us bend down, slow down, and protect little ones and vulnerable ones. The great souls demonstrate humility, simplicity, and yield to instruction. Children always bear the impression of others in their lives. To be great in the kingdom of God is to bear the impression of Jesus who blessed the children and never offended one.

Our false measures of greatness lead us to despise the little ones. In doing so, we despise Christ. To despise a little one is also to despise the angels of heaven and the Eternal God for whom they serve the little ones.

To be great then means to speak out for the little and the vulnerable. It means to expose the deeds of darkness and rescue the oppressed and abused. It means to stop, listen, receive, and act on behalf of the children. It means to know that no mission, no church, no school, no family, and no institution is to allow or conceal the despising of little ones, and that if it does all those who are complicit in that offend both children and Christ. Those who fail to receive one child anywhere at any time are not great no matter their accomplishments but instead are contributing to the destruction of a child, the shrinking of their souls and the marring of the name of the greatest One who ever walked this earth – the one who was born a babe in a manger.

For further thought:

In what ways have you been measuring greatness in your life?

> *"The sphere of Jesus' mission was where His kingdom should be, in the great interior of the heart."*
>
> **Henry Burton**[49]

---

[49] Henry Burton, *The Expositor's Bible: The Gospel According to Luke*, 51.

The Call to Ethical Character

We live in a society that has certain expectations for those in leadership or in the public forum. We expect leaders to be successful, magnetic, powerful, expert, articulate, strong, and on top of things. One of the results is the pressure on those in positions of power or influence to hide anything within themselves or their lives that is contrary to those expectations. The fears, inadequacies, struggles, and suffering go underground and the person in leadership develops a private self that is different from the public self.

The outcome of such split lives is often tragic as we see in sexual abuse crises chronicled over and again in our papers and magazines. Counselors, pastors, priests, and others in the so-called helping professions have carried on a hidden life that has been damaging rather than helpful for the very people they have been called to serve. What are some of the factors that contribute to this ongoing damage?

Elevation of Knowledge

Many graduate schools and seminaries focus on imparting knowledge and skills with little attention given to the instrument that will be wielding that knowledge and skill from a position of power. That means a young adult from an alcoholic family, who was physically abused and has coped by means of high achievement and a pornography addiction, can come to Christ in college, attend a seminary or graduate program where they tack on a tremendous amount of knowledge, make straight A's, graduate, and enter a pulpit having never considered the impact of that history or dealt with either the need to achieve or the addiction.

People whose character is not good and healthy (dare I say, holy?) misuse knowledge. Knowledge breeds arrogance, superiority, and disconnection. According to the Scriptures, those in leadership are to demonstrate love, humility, and service. The character of the person who wields knowledge is every bit as critical as the information itself.

Integrity

Scripture says that those who care for the body of Christ are to be above reproach (1 Timothy 3:2). They are to have integrity. They are not to merely appear righteous, but to actually be so, both in the hidden and the public aspects. Should not God's priority of the character of the worker be the priority of those of us who train others or hire them for positions of leadership?

But oftentimes, we want to maintain the integrity of the role, rather than the integrity of the person. We want the form intact even when there is no integrity in the substance. It is as if we think the worst thing in the world is exposing wrongdoing in someone who previously looked good outwardly.

We forget that God thinks that sin is the worst thing in the world. How we must grieve Him when we work hard to preserve the appearance of godliness without substance. Do we think he cannot see? Do we think he merely wants us to look good to ourselves or to others? Do we really think that we are honoring and pleasing him in the work we do while performing without integrity? Do we think our numbers, our reputations, our book signings, and our accolades serve him who is holy and who desires, not our success, but our humble and contrite hearts?

Power

We can hold great power and not feel powerful. You can feel tired, needy, fragile, and even powerless, and still wield tremendous power. Such things do not remove or dilute our power; they make us more likely to use it destructively. The more needy we feel in a position of power, the more dangerous we are because we are far more likely to use the sheep for food.

There are many different kinds of power. The combination of verbal power, knowledge, skill, position, and emotional sway can all be used in concert to move, manipulate, or convince another human being who is vulnerable. Power can be used to intimidate people so they won't say no to something they would refuse in other circumstances. Power can be used to feed the person in power with something the sheep has.[50]

The Call

I fear sometimes we have lost the call to him. We have forgotten that our primary call is *to* him, not to a task. Our ears have been seduced away by other things, taking our hearts with them. We are not only hurting the sheep as a result; we are breaking the heart of the Shepherd. He does not want our goal to be knowledge, or degrees, or books, or money, or reputation, or success. He wants us to love and obey him. When we understand this and pursue it above all else, the body of Christ will be the safest place on earth for the most vulnerable of sheep.

If we understand this, then we will pursue love and obedience to Christ in our own lives, both public and private. We will understand that he is pleased when we are conformed to His image, not when we are wealthy or successful or famous. We will know that hidden sin in our lives grieves Him more than any other failure. We will know that He cares far more that we look at the mirror He holds up to us so we can see ourselves in truth, than He does for the image we project to the world.

---

[50] Further thoughts on power can be found in "Redeeming Power: Understanding Authority and Abuse in the Church."

The body of Christ alone has access to the cure. It is the supernatural work of the Spirit of God in us. May we who are already in positions of power and influence lead the way by falling down on our faces, imploring God to make us like himself no matter the cost to our positions so that we might work safely among his sheep, looking like him.

For further thought:

In what ways has your life been focused more on the elevation of knowledge, integrity of your role in society, and the search for power rather than the call to live out His truth?

"Looking unto Jesus: staring; a look that suggests amazement; the seeing of something that has completely captured the mind; such complete capture by the thing that all other visions have faded; unmindful of all else. That is the secret of running this great race."

G. Campbell Morgan[51]

---

[51] G. Campbell Morgan, *God's Last Word to Man: Studies in Hebrews* (London: Marshall Morgan & Scott, 1948), 129-130. Used with permission; see References.

Brief Meditation 11

"Every time you make a choice you are turning the central part of you, the part of you that chooses, into something a little different from what it was before. And taking your life as a whole, with all the innumerable choices, all your life long you are slowly turning this central thing wither into a heavenly creature or a hellish creature."

C.S. Lewis[52]

---

[52] C.S. Lewis, *Mere Christianity* (New York, NY: HarperCollins Publishers, 1961), 92. Used with permission; see References.

Brief Meditation 12

"Fungus: lacking chlorophyll and vascular tissue; feeds on organic matter. Our methods are multiplied today and yet one cannot help the conviction that many of our organizations are fungus growths, sapping the church's life and contributing nothing to her fruitfulness."

G. Campbell Morgan[53]

---

[53] G. Campbell Morgan, *The Practice of Prayer* (Grand Rapids, MI: Fleming H. Revell, Co., 1906), 12.

Week 7

Living a Sanctified Life

Abortion has been a focus of the evangelical world for decades now. We have written, spoken, and marched on behalf of the unborn. We have declared – rightly – that every human life is precious and worthy of protection and care. Sadly, such a focus has also often derailed us in our calling to be Christlike.

The word "abort" means to come to nothing. It is anything that fails in its progress before it is matured. To abort is to abandon or terminate that which is not yet fully developed. We have limited the term to one that refers to unborn children. This is certainly one application of the word, and to ignore that is literally life destroying. I fear, however, that from God's perspective, His people have aborted many lives while being simultaneously convinced that they are fiercely protecting life.

We take a stand against the abortion of a pregnancy because we believe that every single human life is eternally precious. We believe the psalmist who says we were knit together in our mother's womb by the hand of the Almighty God (Psalm 139:13 NIV). It is puzzling, then, why we have failed to be equally adamant about protecting human life wherever we find it – in the abused, the trafficked, the immigrant, the widow, and the orphan. Is not our God as concerned about those human lives – lives that were also knit together in their mothers' wombs?

I think our God defines life far more broadly than we do and that from His perspective we abort *his* life within us every time we choose whatever is not like him. Surely when we choose death over life, we have chosen against the One who is life itself. Yet clearly when we choose or ignore injustice, rudeness, and hate filled speech, we are aborting the life of God in us.

It is subtle sometimes. We can be so governed by a good thing – protecting the unborn – that we fail to see that its governance of our lives has led us to abort the life and character of our God in pursuit of our goal. It is good to preserve human life. Let us never forget it. It is good to protect the weak and the vulnerable both inside and outside the womb. However, to do so with rage, hateful language, demeaning words, or scorn means we have in our delivery aborted God's mission. Yes, we are to speak out for the mute, for the rights of all the unfortunate, and protect the weak (Proverbs 31:8, 9 NASB) – but we are to do so perennially bearing his likeness. He who spoke truth boldly, never acted without love.

Single-minded focus on an issue can easily lead us to forget that we will never encounter a human being who was not knit together by God in the womb. We will

never encounter a human being who was not created in
the image of God, shattered though that image may be.
We will never encounter a human being for whom
Christ did not die. Do we grasp that this is as true of
those who oppose us as it is of ourselves? Such singular-
ity of focus can also lead us into thinking that the issue
itself is the great and grand mission of our lives. When
that happens, we will do anything to achieve our goals,
including acting in ways that look nothing like Christ,
all the while using his name to sanction our choices.

The great and grand mission in this world is not
simply to protect the unborn, as significant as that is. It
is far greater than one issue. The great mission of those
belonging to the kingdom of heaven is to never, under
any circumstances or for any goal, abort the life of
Christ in us individually and/or corporately. The kingdom of heaven is the kingdom of the heart, and that
kingdom is come when we see more of God... more of
his power and wisdom and love and holiness evident in
the lives of his children.

Any issue, no matter how close to the heart of our
God, that preempts likeness to him in our lives is an
abortion. We are, as his people, to speak up, pursue
righteousness, protect the afflicted and needy, but we
are to ever and always do so beholding his glory and
transformed into his image. Anything less is an abortion
of God's life and kingdom. Anything less will come to
nothing and has failed in God's eyes because the fragrance of Christ in the life has been extinguished and
the life has not developed into maturity. Any word, any
tone, any choice, and any behavior that is not Christlike

is an abortion of the life of God in us. As we stand for life, may we truly stand for life as God defines it – a likeness to Him in all we are and do.

For further thought:

Meditate on the quote below. Pray for strength and wisdom to speak and live in a way that does not abort his life within us.

> *"May I be enabled to make every lineament of thy spotless character my daily study, so as gradually to be transformed into the same image from glory to glory."*
>
> **John Macduff**[54]

---

[54] John Macduff, *The Morning Watches, and Night* (New York, NY: Robert Carter & Brothers, 1855), 71.

From the Inside Out

The Christian world has been slow to recognize and speak about institutional sin. Perhaps that is the Western influence with its focus on individualism and independence. Institutions are often complicit in, and even condone, evil, while at the same time speak out against it, denying its existence and justifying it when it is exposed. As counselors, we have seen this dynamic play out in family systems. When we work with families where there is domestic violence or sexual abuse, for example, we encounter systems that fight exposure and work hard to preserve the status quo regardless of the cost to the individuals within it. We also know that churches have sometimes colluded with these families, believing that preservation of the system, no matter the evil it contains, is the biblical way.

It is not a big step to understand, then, that larger systems can fight for self-preservation, even while rotting at the center. The Catholic Church has been in the headlines in recent years for preserving itself, protecting its pedophile priests, and thereby allowing hundreds of child victims to spend their lives struggling with the memories and aftereffects of sexual abuse. We have more recently heard about mission organizations and Christian schools that have behaved in a similar fashion, refusing to believe the victims and investigate their reports. And of course, that is not just in "those" churches or "over there." These evils occur regularly in evangelical, Protestant churches in the United States as well. The news reports have made that very clear.

It is ironic how institutions, ordained by God and set up to preserve, protect, defend, and nurture, can end up devouring people in an effort to maintain the larger structure. It is reminiscent of Israel, a nation chosen by God and given rules and teachings so as to preserve *not* simply the institution, but the people within it as well. Israel, as a system, sadly became like the families with which we have often worked. She stood as a nation; her people continued to follow some of the teachings with their sacrifices in the temple and, after a while, she was rotting at the core and destroying the very people she was meant to protect. God's response was to obliterate the institution and scatter the nation like seed. He does not preserve structure with no regard for content. He wants purity in the kingdom of the heart, not the appearance of it in the institution that has to lie to make it seem as if it is present. He would rather the structure be destroyed *so that* He might work in the hearts of broken people and bring transformation from the inside out.

His ways truly are not ours! Think about it. Can you imagine a global church, a mission organization, a

Christian school, a denomination, or a local church finding rottenness and deception in its midst and repenting to the point that the loss of the institution was subservient to obedience to Jesus Christ? What if power and words and resources were all used in concert to bring truth, reconciliation, restitution, and healing for the victims and the constituents? It is not our way. We are afraid. What if we lose all our money? What if we have to close down? We were established for good cause and will lose our opportunities in this world. Our organizations are *not* the kingdom of God. That is not where we will find Him. He resides in the hearts of His people who are called to live in obedience to Him even if it means their structures and institutions fall down around them. We are inclined to obey the institution rather than our God. In doing so, we are disobedient to Him and calling evil good.

Jesus spoke very clearly when He told us that His kingdom *is not* of this world. His kingdom is to be the place where His will is fulfilled. No so-called Christian organization is His kingdom unless all aspects of that institution are governed by His will. So often we have preserved our institutions by pointing to the portion that follows His way, hiding or excusing those places that look nothing like Him; or by using a small part of His Word to justify the evil we allow to continue unhindered and unexposed. The true kingdom of God looks like the King Himself in all His glory.

I pray that we, in this generation, will have the courage to speak the truth about ourselves and our own institutions when they hide sin and pretend

righteousness. I pray that we will bow the knee in repentance when sin is exposed in our families, our
churches, and our organizations. Such a response is the
fabric of revival, something much needed in this land
and this world.

For further thought:

Have you seen the church value the institution
more than obedience to Jesus? Pray for the institutions that exist around us, for wisdom and courage to handle the cases of abuse that may have
occurred, for repentance, and for revival.

> *"Are we wearing His nature as He still wears ours?
> Are we growing more divine as He is changelessly hu-
> man? Are we living a Christ-imitating, Christ-exalting
> life, even as He lived a man-abased, yet man-saving
> life?"*
>
> ***Octavius Winslow**[55]*

---

[55] Octavius Winslow, *The Lord's Prayer: Its Spirit and Its
Teaching* (London: John F. Shaw & Co., 1866), 82-83.

Are We Protecting the Robbers' Dens?

The word sanctuary means a refuge, a shelter, a port in the storm. It originates from the Latin word, "sanctus," which translates as "holy." This means a sanctuary is a place of holiness that is also a refuge for the vulnerable. However, God's Word indicates that his holy sanctuary can be turned into a refuge for robbers... a hiding place for those who are wronging or defrauding others. We know this from two people. One is Jeremiah, who quotes God as saying, "Has this house, which is called by my name, become a den of robbers?" (Jeremiah 7:11 NASB). The second person is Jesus Himself, who displayed His anger when cleansing the sanctuary by turning over tables and driving animals out, saying God's house had been made a robber's den (Matthew 21:13 NIV). By definition, a den is a hiding place for predators or illicit activity. In this case, God's sanctuary sadly becomes a den when it is used to hide predators or wrongdoing.

Both Jeremiah and Jesus spoke these words in the midst of worship and praise and large crowds. These are circumstances we usually view as proof of God's presence and blessing. Under *those* circumstances, in which we usually rejoice, God's people were intentionally crushing the needy and vulnerable. For Jeremiah, the people of Israel were simultaneously worshipping Moloch, a large bronze idol full of fire into which children were sacrificed. The people of God worshipping in his house were, in fact, worshipping with deceptive words and acts of evil as they continued to do to the little ones something God never commanded, and which never even entered his mind (Jeremiah 7:31 NIV). Their behavior in the house of God looked and sounded like worship, but it was in vile disobedience as they sinned against God and His creation. The only refuge they represented was a refuge of lies. A den indeed! The very place meant to be a dwelling of God in the Spirit, a refuge for the weak and hurting, was in need of cleansing. On both occasions, for Jeremiah and Jesus, God ultimately allowed those two magnificent temples to be destroyed when cleansing did not occur.

How is it, then, that we deem it holy to protect institutions over our children, or label marriage sacred when it is full of fear, violence, and abuse? Church sanctuaries and marriages have ceased to be sacred when they have become a hiding place for predators. Where in the Scriptures do we see God sending his sheep *back* to the wolves? Sheep require protection *from* wolves.

Where do we who serve a holy God, full of grace and truth, find justification for protecting a place where he desires to dwell, when that place is full of sin and harm done to his lambs? In doing so, we fail to meet even the requirements of the law of the land, which calls the abuse of children and spouses criminal.

Jesus cleansed the temple twice. His people did not listen. The spiritual leaders of the people failed to obey Him. This desecration of God's house and His people were scathingly denounced by both Jeremiah and Jesus. We the people of God, who worship in his sanctuary, need to pay heed and listen. Our God would have His refuge be holy as He is holy. Any complicity with sin or abuse in the sanctuary is to be joined with those things that make sanctuary a necessity. In the voices of both Jeremiah and Jesus, we hear condemnation and anger... for not only are God's people plundered, his name has also been desecrated and abused.

In Matthew, after Jesus cleansed the temple the second time, he gave us a clear view of his ability to restore God's house to its true calling thereby giving us a picture of what that restoration looks like. After the cleansing, the wounded and sick came in and He healed them. And the little ones came into the temple and sang praises to our God. When the people of God exposure deeds of darkness and the wolves in our midst who commit them, the wounded are healed, and the children sing. Then we will know the sanctuary of our God is indeed a holy dwelling for our Lord's Spirit and a safe harbor for his lambs.

One of the measures of our faithfulness to God is the way we conduct ourselves in relationship to our fellow humans. A second measure of our faithfulness to God is in the stamping out of sins that wrong humanity. Only when these conditions are met do we, as his people, flesh out the character of a holy and loving God to the afflicted and needy in our midst before a watching world. Only then have we become a true sanctuary – a holy and safe place.

For further thought:

Think about your own church, organization, counseling office, or even your own home. In what ways is it a sanctuary? In what ways may it be guilty of being a robber's den?

"If we love our own ideology and our own opinion instead of loving our brother, we will seek only to glorify only our ideas and our institutions and by that fact we will make real communication impossible."

Thomas Merton[56]

---

[56] Thomas Merton, *Faith and Violence: Christian Teaching and Christian Practice* (Notre Dame, IN: Notre Dame Press, 1968).

Tending to the Sick Among Us

The Philadelphia Hospital for Mental Diseases opened for its first patient in 1907. The population grew quickly, as did the stories of abuse and neglect. During World War II, 3,000 conscientious objectors were assigned to mental hospitals around the country. In Philadelphia, a Quaker, named Charlie Lord, was appalled by the conditions of these patients and surreptitiously used three rolls of film to take photos in order to expose the violence and ongoing humiliation inflicted on vulnerable humans. Following World War II, Eleanor Roosevelt and the general public were appalled at the horrific abuse, having just witnessed the decimation of human beings carried out by the Nazi regime. Byberry, as the hospital was called, reached its peak in the 1960s with 7,000 patients. Again in the 80s, horrid living conditions, sexual abuse, and starvation were exposed, and the facility was closed in 1990.

As counselors, many of you have worked with those who have experienced abuse in psychiatric hospitals. You are keenly aware of the shame and ostracism patients have experienced – not only in society at large, but within the Christian community. Some may have family members who have suffered from both a particular diagnosis and the wrongful, hurtful, and ignorant responses of others. To navigate life with a mind inside your head that does not hold on to what is real or torments you day and night is to live with great vulnerability, confusion, pain, and despair. The pictures that Lord took were published in LIFE® magazine and titled "Bedlam 1946." They are deeply distressing; however, improper responses by the Christian community – including its judgments or avoidance of those whose minds are their own enemies, and from which they cannot escape – are equally disturbing.

Certainly, there are also examples of the Church entering in and caring with dignity for those with mental illness, as well as those such as Charlie Lord, who have exposed abuse toward the vulnerable and worked to bring change when human beings were suffering in hidden places. If we are to live in this world as people obedient to the Word of God, then we must live out 1 Corinthians 12:22-23 (NASB), which tells us an outstanding truth: "...those members of the body which seem to be weaker are necessary. Those parts of the body which we think to be less honorable, on those we bestow more abundant honor; and our unpresentable parts have more abundant propriety."

Look at Lord's pictures and see – see the indignity, the dehumanizing "bestowed" on those who were created in the image of God... see the abuse of power against the helpless and those with no voice... see the degradation which not only shames those so dishonored, but also dishonors the name of the Lord our God who created both the vulnerable and the "caregiver." Then let us raise our heads and hearts to those around us. Let us look at our own families where depression, despair, and anxiety cloud minds; where voices torment thoughts; where agitation and sleeplessness lead to irrational thinking. Let us look on the outskirts of our churches where many are marginalized because we have not yet learned how to enter into their pain and wounds and sit silently and respectfully, able to relinquish our own egotistical, misguided need to fix, preach, or heal. Such times with people will grow our humility as finite lovers of God, acknowledging that we find much of the human mind a fallen and mysterious place... including our own. A simple verse or admonition or instruction for greater faith will not cure mental illness. If it was that easy, none of us would struggle with lust or gossip or anger or addiction or obesity because we would simply add an extra dose of faith and be fine ourselves. We are not.

One of the lessons I have learned as a psychologist is that God brings people into our offices, schools, churches, and personal lives to call us into their world, where he has much to teach us. As a student of the traumatized, I can attest to that. I have changed. I see and know God in ways that would never have been possible had he not called me to enter into a place that was foreign to me and one in which I was ill-equipped to respond. Some of that change has come through listening, empathizing, entering in, and sitting with – not with answers and fixes, but presence, dignity, and care.

Is that not God's call to His people? He left honor, dignity, and the central place of power to enter into the lives of the vulnerable, suffering, marginalized, and tormented. If we, as His people, live in this way, will the world not want to know Him? And as so typical of God, if this is our response as his church – and the world sees and is hungry for what they see – then it will be the broken, the confused, the inarticulate, and the disregarded who will have led us all to Him.

For further thought:

Think of the suffering and struggles you have heard about in the world recently. Bring these to God and ask Him what He is trying to teach you through them.

"If God is prepared to risk using a man...then let the man be prepared to risk everything upon God."

G. Campbell Morgan[57]

---

[57] G. Campbell Morgan, *Studies in the Prophecy of Jeremiah,* 91. Used with permission; see References.

Hear the Word of the Lord

The church is suffering greatly – by her own hands. Self-injury, whether by individuals or institutions, invariably involves faulty thinking that is borne out of self-deception. Many of us are grieved at the wreckage in the church that occurs when victims are silenced, abusers are protected, power is abused, and "truth" is disseminated to the less powerful. The body of our Lord is sick. Here are some thoughts for her.

To begin with, it is important to remember that *all* power is derivative. The power that is inherent in one's position, gifting, knowledge, verbal ability, or spiritual authority has one source – *all power comes from Christ.* He said, "*All* power is given to me in heaven *and on earth...*" It is not ours; it is his and is to be used in accord with his word and his character. He who had all power never used it to feed on a vulnerable person, to increase his stature or to protect himself. Any power we have is his and is to be used to bless others with his grace and truth.

Second, God is ever and always, with no shadow or turning, both light and truth. He is truth. He is light. Light exposes the truth. It exposes beauty and horror. Clean and filthy. And truth always calls what is exposed by its right name. "White-washed tombs full of dead men's bones" is both exposure and truth. To cover-up or even slightly shade, deceive or rename anything the light exposes is ungodly. The Light does not flinch. The Truth does not water down. You see it is only light and truth together that expose the cancer; call it by its right name and enable healing to occur.

Third, light and truth require transparency- which simply means letting light pass through so that what is hidden can be distinctly seen. Transparency is the opposite of complicity which means to be folded up with. That means when sin is named, light is needed. We do not like it. Neither did Adam and Eve whose immediate response was to hide. We prefer hiding and damage control. God calls us to the truth and light of transparency. Transparency protects both alleged victims and alleged predators from the horrific burden of lies. A transparent process protects truth for all. When those in power attempt to dissemble in order to protect an institution they are no longer accomplishing damage control. They are causing damage – damage to God's precious sheep and damage to the name of our God – this, in the name of protecting the house of the Lord. That is what the Israelites said in Jeremiah – "the Temple of the Lord" – all the while throwing their children, the vulnerable ones, into the fire of Moloch. God's response was to destroy the temple system he ordained and designed and cast his people across the earth.

Fourth, words matter significantly. To call alleged victims liars is an attempt to determine outcome without knowledge. We are to call things by their right name. And as people of the Book we acknowledge that the human heart is utterly deceitful and our own is incomprehensible to us. That means we do not trust our own motives and hearts. It means we do not automatically assume our leaders, no matter how beloved, are telling the truth. And we certainly do not assume the vulnerable ones are liars.

Fifth, oh we say, but what about God's grace and mercy? It is indeed vast, and I am utterly grateful that I can stand in that myself. However, grace and mercy never, under any circumstances, tolerate sin – for it is the terminal illness that is slaughtering humanity – people God knit together, loves and died for. He will not budge an inch when that disease has a toehold in any human being. Cancer multiplies and spreads and kills. One cell is too much. Tearful apologies are not sufficient – only radical surgery. We fail to love those who abuse when we do not grasp this truth. Sin, like cancer, starts small and spreads and treatment knocks a life over. God's love and mercy, like that treatment, will do the same.

Sixth, God's people are called to humility. That means church leaders must recognize the potential for bias that is inherent in their positions. A fundamental understanding of our own capacity for self-deception requires that we avail ourselves the independent scrutiny of those that are not part of the institution. That also means we see that all power is derivative and that any power used to feed the self in some fashion is not godly – no matter the attendance numbers, the money coming in, the books published, the gifting, the brilliance, or any other thing. Humility bends down, becomes like, leaves glory, washes feet, and ever and only listens to the voice of the Father no matter the cost.

Finally, dear vulnerable ones, those used, silenced, and cast aside – know that Jesus is often not like his church. He loves and calls us to truth and light, transparency and right naming. He himself is the one who bends to tend and care for you when his church does not. He weeps – not only over you and your suffering at the hands of those who name his name – but also over his church saying, as he did over Jerusalem: "If you had known the things that make for your peace...my house has become a den of robbers."

For further thought:

Pray for the leadership of the church, your family, fellow believers, and yourself. Ask the Father to work in your heart, to be more like him, to be humble, and to fix your eyes solely on him.

"The effect of prayer on ourselves is the building up of our character in the understanding of the character of God."

Oswald Chambers[58]

---

[58] Oswald Chambers, *Christian Disciplines: Building Strong Character* (Grand Rapids, MI: Discovery House Publishers., 2013). Used with permission; see References.

References

Carmichael, Amy. *His Thoughts Said...His Father Said* © 1941 by The Dohnavur Fellowship. Used by permission of CLC Publications. All rights reserved.

Chambers, Oswald. *Christian Disciplines: Building Strong Character* © 1995 by Oswald Chambers Publications Assn., Ltd. Used by permission of Discovery House, Grand Rapids, MI. 49501. All rights reserved.

Chambers, Oswald. *My Utmost for His Highest* © 1935 by Dodd Mead & Co., renewed © 1963 by the Oswald Chambers Publications Assn., Ltd. Used by permission of Discovery House, Grand Rapids MI 49501. All rights reserved.

Chesterton, G. K. *The Everyman Chesterton* © 2011 by The Everyman Library. Used by permission of The Everyman Library. All rights reserved.

Lewis, C. S. *Mere Christianity* © 1942, 1943, 1944, 1952 by CS Lewis Pte Ltd. Used by permission of The CS Lewis Company Ltd. All rights reserved.

Morgan, G. Campbell. *The Acts of the Apostles* © 1934 by Morgan, G. Campbell. Used by permission of Wipf and Stock Publishers. www.wipfandstock.com. All rights reserved.

Morgan, G. Campbell. *The Corinthian Letters of Paul: An Exposition on I and II Corinthians* © 1946 by Morgan, G. Campbell. Used by permission of Wipf and Stock Publishers. www.wipfandstock.com. All rights reserved.

Morgan, G. Campbell. *Exposition of the Whole Bible: Chapter by Chapter in One Volume* © 1959 by Morgan, G. Campbell. Used by permission of Wipf and Stock Publishers. www.wipfandstock.com. All rights reserved.

Morgan, G. Campbell. *God's Last Word to Man: Studies in Hebrews* © 1948 by Morgan, G. Campbell. Used by permission of Wipf and Stock Publishers. www.wipfandstock.com. All rights reserved.

Morgan, G. Campbell. *The Gospel According to Mark* © 1927 by Morgan, G. Campbell. Used by permission of Wipf and Stock Publishers. www.wipfandstock.com. All rights reserved.

Morgan, G. Campbell. *The Great Physician: The Method of Jesus with Individuals* © 1937 by Morgan, G. Campbell. Used by permission of Wipf and Stock Publishers. www.wipfandstock.com. All rights reserved.

Morgan, G. Campbell. *Studies in the Prophecy of Jeremiah* © 1955 by Morgan, G. Campbell. Used by permission of Wipf and Stock Publishers. www.wipfandstock.com. All rights reserved.

Schonberg, Harold C. *The Lives of Great Composers* © 1997, 1981, 1970 by Harold C. Schonberg. Used by permission of W. W. Norton & Co. All rights reserved.

Essays

Day 1 – Soldiers of the Kingdom
Previously published in *Christian Counseling Today*,
2012, vol. 19, no. 2.

Day 2 – The Different Parts We Play
Previously published as "The Body – Part 1" in *Christian Counseling Connection*, 2002, vol. 10, no. 1.

Day 3 – The Body of Christ
Previously published as" The Body of Christ – Part Three in a Series of Three" in *Christian Counseling Connection*, 2002, vol. 10, no. 3.

Day 4 – Bringing the Extraordinary into Flesh and Blood
Previously published as "Reflections on Ground Zero" in *The Quarterly of Christian Education and Publications*, 2002, Second Quarter.

Day 5 – Crises Reveal Character
Previously published as "Building Character Through the Crisis of Care" in *Christian Counseling Today*, 2012, vol. 19, no. 4.

Day 8 – The Church as a Sanctuary
Previously published in *Safe Place News*, March 2002, no. 16.

Day 9 – The Deceived Heart
Previously published as "Addiction and the Deceived Heart" in *Christian Counseling Today*, 2016, vol. 22, no. 1.

Day 10 – The Spiritual Cancer Within
Previously published in *Christian Counseling Today*, 2010, vol. 17, no. 4.

Day 11 – To Heal or to Hide
Previously published as "Understanding the Whole Counsel of God" in *Christian Counseling Today*, 2011, vol. 18, no. 2.

Day 12 – The Parable of Rwanda
Previously published as "A Living Parable: The Message of Rwanda" in *Christian Counseling Today*, 2014, vol. 21, no. 1.

Day 15 – The Weak Strengthens the Strong
Previously published as "The Body – Part 2" in *Christian Counseling Connection*, 2002, vol. 10, no. 2.

Day 16 – Feeding the Hungry
Previously published as "Feeding the Hungry: From Tragedy to Opportunity" in *Christian Counseling Today*, 2009, vol. 17, no. 1.

Day 17 – The Human Will
Previously published in *Christian Counseling Today*, 2009, vol. 16, no. 3.

Day 18 – And a Little Child Shall Lead Them
Previously published in *Christian Counseling Today*,
2013, vol. 20, no. 2.

Day 19 – Intimacy with God
Previously published in *Christian Counseling Today*,
2009, vol. 16, no. 4.

Day 22 – Our Composer and Our Marriages
Excerpted from "Marriage: A Two-Voice Invention" in
Marriage & Family: A Christian Journal, 1999, vol. 2, no.
1.

Day 23 – Harmonious Voices
Excerpted from "Marriage: A Two-Voice Invention" in
Marriage & Family: A Christian Journal, 1999, vol. 2, no.
1.

Day 24 – Serving God in His House
Previously published in *Christian Counseling Today*,
2011, vol. 18, no. 4.

Day 25 – Challenging the Culture by Having the Mind
of Christ
Previously published in *Christian Counseling Today*,
2013, vol. 20, no. 3.

Day 26 – The Least of These
Previously published on dianelangberg.com, 15 July
2019.
http://www.dianelangberg.com/2019/07/the-least-of-
these/.

Day 29 – Lessons from the Every Day
Previously published as "Golf Carts, Wheelchairs and
Famous Men" in *Christian Counseling Today*, 2006, vol.
14, no. 2.

Day 30 – Three-Legged Race
Previously published in *Christian Counseling Today*,
2017, vol. 22, no. 2.

Day 31 – Divisions, Deceptions and Disease
Previously published on dianelangberg.com, 27 August
2018.
http://www.dianelangberg.com/2018/08/divisions-de-
ceptions-disease/.

Day 32 – The Forces that Shape Us
Previously published in *Christian Counseling Today*,
1997, vol. 5, no. 4.

Day 33 – Breaking Faith or Bearing Fruit?
Previously published in *Christian Counseling Today*,
2019, vol. 23, no. 4.

Day 36 – Going by Way of the Cross
Previously published as "The Spiritual Life of the Therapist: We Become What We Habitually Reflect" in *Journal of Psychology & Christianity*, 2006, vol. 25, no. 3.

Day 37 – Yielding to the Lordship of Christ
Previously published as "Leadership: Yielding to the
Lordship of Christ" in *Christian Counseling Today*, 2010,
vol. 17, no. 4.

Day 38 – When the Prince of Peace Calls
Previously published in *Christian Counseling Today*,
2014, vol. 20, no. 4.

Day 39 – Measuring Greatness in the Kingdom of God
Previously published as "Measuring Greatness: Children
and the Kingdom of God" in *Religion News Service*, 8
August 2014.
https://religionnews.com/2014/08/08/measuring-
greatness-children-kingdom-god/.

Day 40 – The Call to Ethical Character
Previously published as "Sexual Abuse and the Call to
Ethical Character" in *Christian Counseling Today*, 2005,
vol. 12, no. 4.

Day 43 – Living a Sanctified Life
Previously published in *Christian Counseling Today*,
2011, vol. 19, no. 1.

Day 44 – From the Inside Out
Previously published as "Integrity from the Inside Out"
in *Christian Counseling Today*, 2009, vol. 17, no. 2.

Day 45 – Are We Protecting the Robber's Dens?
Previously published as "Sanctuary or Robber's Den" in
Christian Counseling Today, 2018, vol. 23, no, 1.

Day 46 – Tending to the Sick Among Us
Previously published in *Christian Counseling Today*,
2015, vol. 21, no. 2.

Day 47 – Hear the Word of the Lord
Previously published as "Dear Church: Hear the Word
of the Lord" on dianelangberg.com, 16 April 2018.
http://www.dianelangberg.com/2018/04/dear-
church/

About the Author

Dr. Diane Langberg is globally recognized for her 50 years of clinical work with trauma victims. She has trained caregivers on six continents in responding to trauma and to the abuse of power. For 29 years, she directed her own practice in Jenkintown PA, *Diane Langberg PhD, and Associates*. Now in partnership with Dr. Monroe, Langberg, Monroe & Associates continues this work which includes seventeen therapists with multiple specialties. Dr. Langberg's newest book is Redeeming Power: Understanding Authority and Abuse in the Church. Other books include Counseling Survivors of Sexual Abuse, On the Threshold of Hope (with accompanying workbook), In Our Lives First: Meditations for Counselors and Suffering the Heart of God: How Trauma Destroys and Christ Restores.

Dr. Langberg is the recipient of the Distinguished Alumna Achievements from Taylor University., the American Association of Christian Counselors Caregiver Award, The Distinguished President's award, and the Philadelphia Council of Clergy's Christian Service Award.

She is married and has two sons and four grandchildren.

Other Books by Diane Langberg

For a complete list of works by Dr. Langberg, please visit: https://www.dianelangberg.com/shop-books/

Redeeming Power: Understanding Authority and Abuse in the Church (*Brazos Press, 2020*)

On the Threshold of Hope: Opening the Door to Hope and Abuse (*Tyndale House Publishing, 1999*)

On the Threshold of Hope Workbook (*Xulon Press, 2014*)

Counseling Survivors of Sexual Abuse (*Xulon Press, 2003*)

Suffering and the Heart of God (*New Growth Press, 2015*)

In Our Lives First: Meditations for Counselors Volume 1 (2013)

Made in United States
North Haven, CT
28 April 2024